AF335491

Malcolm Lowry

A BIBLIOGRAPHY

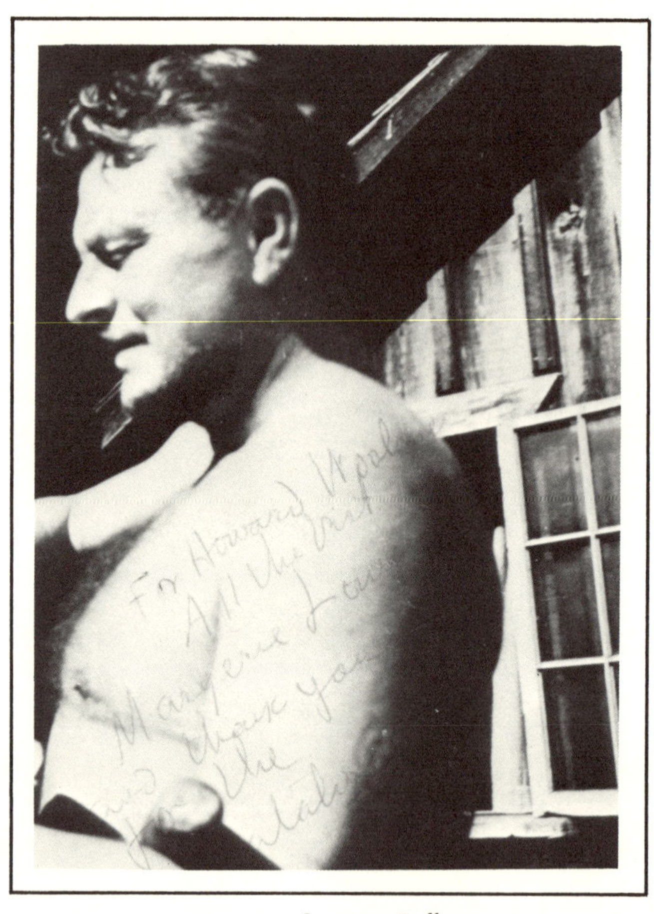

Lowry at Dollarton, Summer 1953

MALCOLM LOWRY

A Bibliography

J. Howard Woolmer

WOOLMER/BROTHERSON LTD
REVERE, PENNSYLVANIA
1983

Published by
WOOLMER/BROTHERSON LTD
REVERE, PENNSYLVANIA 18953

First printing.

Library of Congress Card Number: 82-050810
ISBN: 0-913506-12-5

Printed and bound in the United States of America

For Robert Brotherson
who introduced me to the *Volcano*

CONTENTS

INTRODUCTION

The two series of author bibliographies that I have used as my basis for format are the Soho Bibliographies originally published by Rupert Hart-Davis in London and the Pittsburgh Series in Bibliography, University of Pittsburgh Press. It would be very difficult indeed to improve on these but every bibliographer has his own prejudices based on his own use of bibliographies and I hope that any variations from these two series in this book will add to its ease of use.

The major weakness of this bibliography is the lack of production information for a number of books described in the A and B sections. As more and more publishing firms have merged or been taken over by conglomerates this information has become much more difficult, and in some instances impossible, to obtain. Records have been stored in distant places or, as in the case of firms absorbed by other firms a number of years ago, they seem to have been lost altogether. It would also seem, in some instances, that assigning an employee to spend several hours digging up details on the number of copies that were printed of a particular book is no longer considered justifiable from a budgetary viewpoint.

It is now common practice for publishers to issue advance copies in plain or printed wrappers or, in some cases, to use the dust jacket as wrapper, both for in-house use and for review purposes. These have been noted when I have seen them or seen copies described in booksellers' catalogues. I feel that it is safe to assume that such copies exist for all *cloth* editions at least, with the possible exception of the 1933 edition of *Ultramarine*, even though some publishers deny their existence. The fact that an advance copy is *not* noted in this bibliography does not mean that copies do not exist.

There is no cut-off date for this bibliography. I hope that I have been able to locate everything that has been published up to the date of this writing, but I would be most grateful to anyone who can point out anything that I have missed. I have followed each poem, short story, and article to its first book printing but have not noted these when they appear in anthologies after their first book appearance. Letters from Lowry that appear in *Selected Letters* (1965) have not, of course, been indexed here, but letters published before that date are indexed, as are letters, or excerpts of letters, appearing for the first time after that date.

As with many authors there are ghosts in the Malcolm Lowry canon. I have in my collection a xerox of a letter from Clarisse Francillon to Lowry dated 23 February 1950 in which she states that "The daily paper COMBAT is going to publish the *VOLCAN* as a serial. For that they will pay frs. 20,000 that your editors will leave entirely to you and keep here for you until you come back to France. . . . " I have examined every issue of *Combat* for the years 1950 and 1951 and *Volcan* never appeared although *Combat* did carry other serialized novels during this period.

Again, in a letter to Clarisse Francillon dated 16 February 1948 (*Selected Letters*, p. 166), Lowry mentions a translation by (Andre?) Gide and others of his first book. The only French translation of *Ultramarine* was of the revised, 1962, edition, and it was done by Miss Francillon and Jean-Roger Carroy and published in 1965 (D12).

There has been talk about Lowry working on film scripts during his stay in Hollywood. John Davenport contradicts this, however, (as reported in Day's *Malcolm Lowry*, p. 213) and I have found nothing to indicate that Lowry worked on any script other than F. Scott Fitzgerald's *Tender Is the Night* (A13).

Major manuscript and letter depositories are listed by William H. New in his *Malcolm Lowry: A Reference Guide* (G. K. Hall & Co., 1978). To this list should be added The McFarlin Library, University of Tulsa, which has an important collection of unpublished letters and some manuscript material. Columbia

University Library is now the depository for the papers of the Harold Matson Agency, which contain a number of letters from Margerie Lowry as well as the typescript of *Through the Panama.*

It is interesting to note that despite the lukewarm reception originally given to *Under the Volcano* in his native England, Penguin Books is the only publisher to keep all of Lowry's prose in print.

Section A contains all books and pamphlets by Malcolm Lowry. In describing binding colors I have used the identifying descriptions and numbers in the ISCC-NBS Centroid Color Charts issued by the National Bureau of Standards, U.S. Department of Commerce. It can be assumed that all edges are trimmed unless otherwise noted.

Section B lists contributions by Lowry to books by, or edited by, others. First book appearances only are listed; anthology appearances are not included unless they are the first book printing. Dust jacket blurbs have been included in this section, as have books that contain quotes from Lowry's unpublished works.

Section C contains contributions to periodicals as well as the two interviews that Lowry gave to English newspapers before his first sea voyage and after his return. It also contains quotations from Lowry's writings that appear in booksellers' or auction catalogues. Each entry is listed under title in capitals when there is a title. When a poem is untitled the first line is in lower case within square brackets. When the title of a poem has been supplied by an editor, the entry is in capitals within square brackets. Lowry's reports on hockey games in *The Leys Fortnightly* are listed as "reports on school hockey games" and the individual games are listed in the entry. Lowry signed these reports with his initials, C.M.L. His other contributions to *The Leys Fortnightly* are signed with his pseudonym, "Camel," derived from these initials. It should be noted here that there are cases of the same poem being published under different titles. Cross references are here made for these poems.

Section D contains translations of Lowry's work into foreign languages.

Section E contains radio and television programs and films. I have included all of these, even when they do not contain readings or quotations from Lowry's works, as it seems worthwhile to keep a record of all of these in one place.

Section F contains the song lyrics published by Lowry in London in 1927.

Section G contains the recordings made by Graham Collier. Both albums have been included for convenience even though the first is strictly instrumental.

ACKNOWLEDGMENTS

No bibliography could be compiled without the assistance and cooperation of numerous librarians, booksellers, publishers, and private collectors. Anyone who has been inadvertently left out of the following list has my sincere apologies.

Allen Ahearn, Quill & Brush; Jeffrey Akard, A.B.I. Books; Betty Amster, Random House, Inc.; Gordon Bowker; Prof. M. C. Bradbrook; Mrs. Madeline Braidwood, Clarke Irwin & Co. Ltd.; George Brandak, Special Collections, University of British Columbia Library; Ernest Braund, Library of Congress; Frederick Buechner; William R. Cagle, Lilly Librarian, Indiana University; Cambridge University Library; Eleanor Carlucci, Alfred A. Knopf, Inc.; Frank J. Carroll, Library of Congress; Chloe's Bookstore; C. E. Frazer Clark, Jr.; Susan Clark, Press Porcepic; Bob Clarke, CBC-TV Record Centre, Toronto; Alan Clodd; Mrs. Louis Henry Cohn, House of Books, Ltd.; Joanna Cruddas, Macmillan, Ltd., London; Alyce Cresap for typesetting; Lawrence N. Crumb, Reference Department, University of Oregon Library; Kenneth W. Duckett, Curator of Special Collections, University of Oregon Library; Robert Duncan, National Film Board of Canada; Mel Edelstein; Carola Edmond, New English Library; Allan Ferris, Play Librarian, Radio, BBC London; Robert J. Fiene, Wilder Books; Jo Goldberg, Holt, Rinehart and Winston; Annette Gosselin, Le Club Francais du Livre, Paris; Robert D. Graff; Charles Granade, J. B. Lippincott Company; Jules Greenblatt; David Grusenmeyer, University of Chicago Press; Mrs. Vickie Harkness, General Publishing Co. Ltd., Toronto; Victoria L. Harris, McGraw-Hill Paperbacks; James D. Hart, Director, The Bancroft Library; Christopher Hawtree,

Editorial Assistant, London Magazine; William Hoffer; David Holmes; Glenn Horowitz; Maurice F. Howard; Janet Hughes, Penguin Books; Tim Inkster; Patrick Jamieson, Sandpiper Books; Anne Janowitz, City Lights Books; Kenneth A. Lohf, Librarian for Rare Books and Manuscripts, Columbia University Libraries; Margerie Lowry for her assistance, encouragement, and patience; Richard M. Ludwig, Assistant University Librarian for Rare Books and Special Collections, Firestone Library, Princeton University; Margaret Lyons, Managing Director, CBC Radio Toronto; David Markson; J. Marnham, The Leys School; Miss P. R. Marsh, Cambridge University Press; Mrs. Connie Masters, Audience Services, CBC Toronto; William Matheson, Chief, Rare Books and Special Collections, Library of Congress; Peter H. Matson, Harold Matson Co. Inc.; P. S. Morrish, Brotherton Library; Betty Moss; Jean Mossop, Jonathan Cape Limited; Anton Myrer; Josephus Nelson, Library of Congress; William H. New; The New York Public Library and staff, a great treasure in our midst; Brian O'Kill; Jean Peters; Nancy J. Peters, City Lights Books; Ruth Pickholtz, J. B. Lippincott Company; Omar S. Pound; Richard Q. Praeger, Transition Books; Jack Ramsay, Correspondence Editor, *The Vancouver Sun*; Miss Challice B. Reed, Script Librarian, BBC London; William E. Reinhardt, Book-of-the-Month Club, Inc.; Kathleen E. Richards, Macmillan of Canada; Angela Rinaldi, The New American Library; Bertram Rota Ltd.; W. J. Rowe, Her Majesty's Stationery Office; Dr. G. Sabbagh; Joachim Sartorius; Peter B. Scaggs, McClelland and Stewart Limited, Toronto; Richard Schaubeck; Richard Seaver, Penguin Books; Serendipity Books; J. C. Sharp; Mrs. Jeanne Sheriff, Jonathan Cape Limited; Prof. Harold P. Simonson; Mrs. Norah Smallwood, Chatto and Windus Ltd.; Sandra Soames, G. P. Putnam's Sons; Jeffrey D. Stelmach, Harper & Row, Publishers, Inc.; Marie Stephen, University of British Columbia Press; Roger Stoddard, The Houghton Library; Kaniz Sumar, Oxford University Press, Toronto; Steven Temple Books; Prof. Paul Tiessen, editor, *Malcolm Lowry Newsletter*; Vision Press Limited; Larry Wallrich, About Books; Ann Waterfall, The New American Library; Grace Wherry, Harold Matson Company, Inc.; Yale University Library for the loan of the film of the Paris newspaper *Combat*; and especially Mrs. Anne Yandle, Head of Special Collections, University of British Columbia, and her staff, whose kindness, cooperation, patience, and hospitality will always be remembered.

Apart from individuals, the published work of others always plays an important part in the compiling of a bibliography. The first attempt at a bibliography of Malcolm Lowry was made by Earle Birney with the assistance of Margerie Lowry; it was published in *Canadian Literature* numbers 8 and 9 (Spring and Summer 1961) with supplements appearing in numbers 11 and 19 (Winter 1962 and Winter 1964). The information contained in these issues was of great help. The books that I found most helpful were Douglas Day's *Malcolm Lowry: A Biography* (N.Y.: Oxford University Press, 1973), *The Selected Letters of Malcolm Lowry* edited by Harvey Breit & Margerie Bonner Lowry (Philadelphia: J. B. Lippincott Company, 1965), and William H. New's highly recommended *Malcolm Lowry: A Reference Guide* (Boston: G. K. Hall & Co., 1978).

SECTION A
Books
and
Pamphlets

A. Books and Pamphlets

A1 ULTRAMARINE

A1a: First edition, 1933

ULTRAMARINE

A Novel

BY

MALCOLM LOWRY

JONATHAN CAPE
THIRTY BEDFORD SQUARE
LONDON

A1a: $7\frac{1}{2} \times 4\frac{13}{16}$ inches

FIRST PUBLISHED 1933

JONATHAN CAPE LTD., 30 BEDFORD SQUARE, LONDON
AND 91 WELLINGTON STREET WEST, TORONTO

PRINTED IN GREAT BRITAIN BY J. AND J. GRAY, EDINBURGH
PAPER MADE BY JOHN DICKINSON AND CO. LTD.
BOUND BY A. W. BAIN AND CO. LTD.

[1–12] 13–275 [276–280]

Contents: [1–2]: blank; [3]: half title; [4]: blank; [5]: title page; [6]: copyright; [7]: dedication; [8]: blank; [9]: quotation from Chaucer; [10]: blank; [11]: second half title; [12]: blank; 13–[276]: text; [277–280]: blank.

Binding: Medium blue (182) cloth lettered horizontally on spine in white "ULTRA- | MARINE | MALCOLM | LOWRY | JONATHAN | CAPE" and with publisher's logo blindstamped at upper center of back cover. White endpapers. Bottom edge untrimmed.

Dust jacket: Coated white paper printed in blue and black. See illustration.

Publication: Published 12 June 1933 at 7*s*6*d.* Production records not available, but see *Note* below.

Note: Michael S. Howard, in his *Jonathan Cape, Publisher* (London: Cape, 1971) p. 211, states that 1,500 copies were published but that barely half were sold. A note on the copyright page of the revised edition (London: Cape, 1963) states that *Ultramarine* was reissued in 1935. Cape has no records of this reissue, but the *English Catalogue of Books* lists a "cheap edition" issued in September 1935. I haven't been able to locate a copy but I believe that they were copies of the first edition that were reduced in price rather than a new edition. This was a common practice in the 1930s. See as well the note to the Cape edition of *Under the Volcano*, A2c.

Dust jacket for A1b

A1b: First American, and first revised, edition, 1962

ULTRAMARINE

A NOVEL BY MALCOLM LOWRY

J. B. LIPPINCOTT COMPANY

PHILADELPHIA AND NEW YORK

A1b: $7\frac{15}{16} \times 5\frac{1}{4}$ inches

FIRST AMERICAN EDITION

An earlier version of this novel was published in England in 1933 by Jonathan Cape Ltd.

Printed in the United States of America

Library of Congress Catalog Card Number 62-15207

[1–4] 5–8 [9–12] 13–45 [46] 47–77 [78] 79–127 [128] 129–173 [174] 175–203 [204–208]

Contents: [1]: half title; [2]: *"Also by Malcolm Lowry"* (two titles); [3]: title page; [4]: copyright; 5–8: "Introductory Note" by Margerie Lowry; [9]: second half title; [10]: blank; [11]: quotations from Chaucer and Samuel Richardson; [12]: blank; 13–45: text; [46]: blank; 47–77: text; [78]: blank; 79–127: text; [128]: blank; 129–173: text; [174]: blank; 175–203: text; [204–208]: blank.

Binding: Gray blue (186) cloth lettered horizontally on top cover in light blue "ULTRAMARINE" above a decorative rule. Lettered horizontally on spine, "[*purplish blue*] (five decorative rules) I [*light blue*] ULTRA- I MARINE I [*purplish blue*] (five decorative rules) I [*light blue*] MALCOLM I LOWRY I LIPPINCOTT." Blue endpapers. Fore edge untrimmed.

Dust jacket: Coated white paper lettered in black and white on a blue and white photograph of breaking waves on front panel and spine. Back panel and flaps printed in black and blue on a white ground.

Publication: Published 5 September 1962 at $4.95. Production records not available.

Note: This new edition incorporates the changes Lowry made in his own copy of the original edition.

Dust jacket for A1c

A1c: Revised edition, first British edition, 1963

MALCOLM LOWRY

ULTRAMARINE

a novel

JONATHAN CAPE

THIRTY BEDFORD SQUARE LONDON

A1c: $7\frac{3}{4} \times 5\frac{1}{8}$ inches

AN EARLIER VERSION OF THIS NOVEL WAS FIRST PUBLISHED
BY JONATHAN CAPE LIMITED IN 1933
REISSUED 1935

*

A NEW AND REVISED EDITION
FIRST PUBLISHED IN GREAT BRITAIN 1963
© 1962 BY MARGERIE BONNER LOWRY

PRINTED IN GREAT BRITAIN BY
LATIMER, TREND AND CO. LTD., WHITSTABLE
ON PAPER MADE BY JOHN DICKINSON AND CO. LTD.
BOUND BY A. W. BAIN AND CO. LTD., LONDON

Contents and pagination: Same as in American edition but lacking last two blank leaves.

Binding: Gray blue (186) paper boards lettered horizontally in gilt on spine "MALCOLM | LOWRY | ULTRA- | MARINE | (publisher's logo)." White endpapers. Top edge stained blue.

Dust jacket: Coated white paper lettered in black and white on a blue and white photograph of breaking waves on front panel and spine (same as front panel and spine of American jacket, except for the publisher's logo at bottom of spine). Black and white photograph of Lowry on a blue ground on back panel. Flaps lettered in black on a white ground.

Publication: 4,000 copies published 11 February 1963 at 21*s*. Second and third printings of 1,000 copies each in July 1963 and October 1969.

Note: Reproduced photographically from the American edition. One sentence in the Introductory Note has been deleted in this edition.

Note: See A1a *Note* for discussion of the supposed 1935 reissue.

●

A1d: Canadian edition, 1963

Jonathan Cape supplied Clarke, Irwin & Company Limited with 2,000 copies in 1963. They were priced at $4.00, but approximately 800 were remaindered in 1966. They are identical to the English edition, with the exception of the imprint and price and two changes on the copyright page: "first published in Canada in 1963" and the deletion of the "reissued 1935" note.

●

A1e: McGraw-Hill (paperback) edition, 1964

(Decorative flower) | Ultramarine | Malcolm Lowry | McGraw-Hill Book Company | New York

8 × 5 5/16 inches

[1–4] 5–8 [9–12] 13–45 [46] 47–77 [78] 79–127 [128] 129–173 [174] 175–203 [204–208]

Contents: [1]: descriptive blurb; [2]: *"Also by Malcolm Lowry"* (two titles); [3]: title page; [4]: copyright; 5–8: "Introductory Note" by Margerie Lowry; [9]: half title; [10]: blank; [11]: quotes from Chaucer and Samuel Richardson; [12]: blank; 13–203: text; [204–207]: blank; [208]: "catalog."

Binding: Strong green blue (169) paper wrappers printed in white and green with a face design on front cover created by a photomontage of black shadows against a blue and white aerial photograph of the sea.

Publication: Published 1964 in an edition of 6,000 copies at $1.95; out of print in 1969. "First McGraw-Hill Paperback Edition, 1964" on copyright page.

A1f: Four Square (paperback) edition, 1965

Ultramarine | MALCOLM LOWRY | (publisher's logo) | A FOUR SQUARE BOOK

7 1/8 × 4 1/4 inches

[1–4] 5–160

Contents: [1]: half title; [2]: blank; [3]: title page; [4]: copyright; 5–7: "Introductory Note" by Margerie Lowry; 8: quotes from Chaucer and Samuel Richardson; 9–160: text.

Binding: Paper wrappers lettered in black, red, and purple on a background painting of a freighter in blue, black, and white on front cover; spine and back cover lettered in red, black, and white on a purple background.

Publication: Published September 1965 at 3*s*6*d.* Production records not available. Printing noted on copyright page.

A1g: Penguin Modern Classics (paperback) edition, 1974

MALCOLM LOWRY | ULTRAMARINE | a novel | (publisher's logo) | PENGUIN BOOKS

7 1/8 × 4 5/16 inches

[1–6] 7–10 [11–14] 15–187 [188–192]

Contents: [1]: descriptive blurb; [2]: blank; [3]: quotes from reviews; [4]: blank; [5]: title page; [6]: copyright; 7–10: "Introductory Note" by Margerie Lowry; [11]: half title; [12]: blank; [13]: quotes from Chaucer and Samuel Richardson; [14]: blank; 15–187: text; [188]: blank; [189]: advertisements; [190]: blank; [191–192]: advertisements.

Binding: Paper wrappers lettered in black on a background painting of two ships at sea in blues, green, and brown on front cover; spine and back cover lettered in black and white on a green background.

Publication: 15,000 copies printed in April 1974 at 35*p*. Reissued in July 1975, 13,000 copies, and in August 1980, 15,000 copies. Printings noted on copyright page.

Malcolm Lowry

MALCOLM LOWRY was born in 1909 in Merseyside, England. He was educated at Cambridge, which he left to go to sea. He has shipped to sea many times and might have been found at various periods in his life in China, Russia, the Barbados, Paris, Mexico, and British Columbia. While at Cambridge some of his first work as a writer was published by Edward J. O'Brien in his *Best Short Stories*. In 1932 he took his B.A. at Cambridge and published his first novel, *Ultramarine*. *Under the Volcano* was originally written in the late 30's. Since then it has been entirely rewritten twice, and finished to the author's satisfaction on Christmas Eve of 1944. He is married to the writer Margerie Bonner. They live at present in British Columbia.

Advance critical acclaim:

ALFRED KAZIN:

The book obviously belongs with the most original and creative novels of our time. I feel like paying homage to Lowry — all the more because there is such clear evidence in the book of deliberate self-mastery. His ability to convey in a single texture the different levels of consciousness and the effect upon them all of the Mexican landscape as a stage of the human soul seems to me one of the most remarkable achievements in modern fiction. But I think I understand as well that this is not only a profoundly sustained history of a man's disintegration, but also a positive statement in *defense* ok basic human values and human hope; and that it is the best sense a novel of the politics of men.

ROBERT PENN WARREN:

Malcolm Lowry has written an ambitious and compelling book. Few novelists I know can create an atmosphere and pace a story as well as he. And at the same time his book has a solid intellectual substructure. *Under the Volcano* is a memorable performance . . .

CONRAD AIKEN:

Let us all give humble and grateful thanks that we can once again, after a long walk in the desert of contemporary prose, salute a novelist who can really *write*. Malcolm Lowry's *Under the Volcano* must be, for anyone who loves the English language, a sheer joy. Here it is, all renewed and alive again, a changeable shot-silk sun-shot medium of infinite flexibility, which can adapt itself to the subtlest shade of perception or mood, or suffuse with the bloodiest of horrors, or vanish upwards in air like the most mystical of rope-tricks. There is no contemporary writer who could not learn from this book: it should send us all scuttling back to our workshops. And I mean *all!*

STEPHEN SPENDER:

Malcolm Lowry's *Under the Volcano* is the most interesting novel I have read since Lawrence and Joyce.

Reynal & Hitchcock, 8 West 40th Street, New York City, 18

Under the Volcano

by

Reynal & Hitchcock

Under the Volcano

A NOVEL BY

$3.00

NOTICE: *on the back of this jacket are printed examples of the critical acclaim this novel has received.*

Under the Volcano

by Malcolm Lowry

Under the Volcano is a novel of major importance, one that will be read and re-read, discussed and studied, not only in the year of its first publication, but for years to come.

The story, which is enacted against the glittering background of Mexico on a feast day, is chiefly that of Geoffrey Firmin — formerly a British consul, but now with no occupation except his fabulous drinking — and of his efforts to rise to the occasion of the unexpected return, in the early morning of The Day of the Dead, of his estranged wife Yvonne. His half-brother Hugh, and his boyhood friend Jacques Laruelle, both of whom are in love with Yvonne, are the other principal actors in this dark drama of a man's inability to defeat the sinister forces in himself or to seize the opportunities offered him to save himself. (The first chapter takes place one year later than the main action, and in it all the important themes of the novel are introduced.)

Under the Volcano is a tense and dramatic narrative at its surface level, but the reader will be aware of the deeper significances of which the characters and their actions are symbolic.

Dust jacket for A2a

A2 UNDER THE VOLCANO

A2a: First edition, 1947

Malcolm Lowry

Under the Volcano

Reynal & Hitchcock, New York

A2a: 8 × 5 1/4 inches

Copyright 1947 by Malcolm Lowry

All rights reserved, including the right to reproduce this book, or portions thereof, in any form.

PRINTED IN THE U.S.A. I BY THE CORNWALL PRESS, INC.

[i–vi] [1–2] 3–375 [376–378]

Contents: [i]: half title; [ii]: blank; [iii]: title page; [iv]: copyright; [v]: dedication; [vi]: blank; [1]: second half title; [2]: quotations from

Sophocles, John Bunyan, and Goethe; 3–375: text; [376]:blank; [377]: text; [378]: blank.

Binding: Light gray (264) cloth, lettered in red on top cover "Under the | Volcano" and horizontally on spine "Under the | Volcano | by | Malcolm | Lowry | Reynal & | Hitchcock." White endpapers.

Dust jacket: Coated white paper lettered in yellow, white, and red on a black and white vortex design background on front panel and spine. Lettered in red and black on a white ground on back panel and flaps. First edition dust jacket has quotes from advance reviews by Alfred Kazin, Robert Penn Warren, Conrad Aiken, and Stephen Spender. Later printings quote these plus press reviews.

Publication: Published 19 February 1947 at $3.00. Production records not available, but went into three printings under this imprint; later printings indicated on copyright page.

Note: Advance copies for review were bound in brown paper wrappers printed in black "UNDER THE VOLCANO | A NOVEL BY MALCOLM LOWRY | PROOF COPY" on top cover. I have also seen a copy in plum binder's cloth with a white label printed in black as above.

Note: In Michael Howard's *Jonathan Cape, Publisher* (London: Cape, 1971), the author states that Lowry allowed Reynal & Hitchcock to edit the manuscript of *Under the Volcano* extensively, whereas Jonathan Cape simply asked him for an explanatory preface. After a side by side reading of the American and English editions I have found no differences that cannot be accounted for by copy editing. In some cases, American spellings are used in one edition and English spellings in the other, but not consistently; the English edition uses single quotation marks, whereas the American uses double quotation marks; there are a number of minor punctuation differences and there are several instances of word transposition; in the American edition (p. 338), the barman, a child nicknamed A Few Fleas, "suddenly went out for change," whereas in the English edition (p. 356), he "suddenly went out for a change." The only serious difference that I noted was that the 'rule' ending the first chapter and beginning the second in the American edition was not used in the English edition where the first chapter ends with a simple period and the second begins with three dots.

Note: An excerpt from *Under the Volcano* (N.Y.: Reynal & Hitchcock, 1947, 121–122) was published in *Skookum Wawa Writings of the Canadian Northwest,* edited by Gary Geddes (Toronto: OUP, 1975) under the title "The Most Terrific Place in the World." 10,000 copies were printed 30 October 1975 at $7.50.

Note: Lowry's original title for *Under the Volcano* was *The Valley of the Shadow of Death* while his working title for his whole series of novels was *The Voyage That Never Ends.*

●

A2b: Book-of-the-Month Club Alternate, May 1947

Copy not seen by the bibliographer. The Club has no production records going back this far but advises that the book was identical with the trade edition with the exception that the dust jacket would not have had a price and would have mentioned the Club. There might also have been a blind binder's identification mark on the back cover. Book-of-the-Month Club reissued the book in 1973–74. Roughly 2,500 copies were printed in late 1973 and 1,500 more in early 1974. Both printings were manufactured by the Hadden Craftsmen of Scranton, Pa., and carry the square blind stamp on back cover. This reissue contains the Stephen Spender introduction.

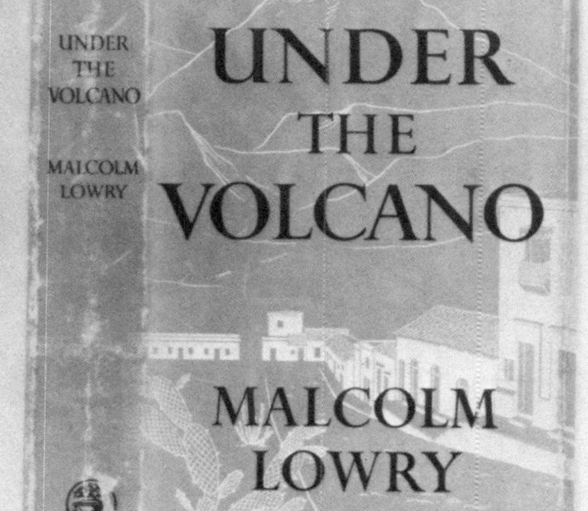

Dust jacket for A2c

A2c: First British edition, 1947

UNDER
THE VOLCANO

by

MALCOLM LOWRY

JONATHAN CAPE
THIRTY BEDFORD SQUARE
LONDON

A2c: $7\frac{1}{2} \times 4\frac{5}{8}$ inches

FIRST PUBLISHED 1947

PRINTED IN GREAT BRITAIN IN THE CITY OF OXFORD
AT THE ALDEN PRESS
BOUND BY A. W. BAIN & CO. LTD., LONDON

[1–4] 5 [6–8] 9–395 [396–400]

Contents: [1]: half title; [2]: blank; [3]: title page; [4]: copyright; 5: quotations from Sophocles, John Bunyan, and Goethe; [6]: dedication; [7]:

second half title; [8]: blank; 9–395: text; [396]: blank; [397]: text; [398–400]: blank.

Binding: Blue gray (191) cloth lettered in red on top cover "Malcolm Lowry I UNDER THE VOLCANO I (decorative rule)" and horizontally on spine in a red decorative rectangle, in gray, "Malcolm I Lowry I (rule) I UNDER I THE I VOLCANO" and with publisher's logo at base of spine. White endpapers. Bottom edge untrimmed.

Dust jacket: White paper lettered in red on pictorial background of a Mexican village in gray and white that extends over front panel and spine. Front flap lettered in red; back panel and flap blank.

Publication: Published 1 September 1947 at 9*s*6*d*. Production records not available.

Note: Michael S. Howard, in his *Jonathan Cape, Publisher* (London: Cape, 1971), states that 5,000 copies were printed and bound and that in 1950 the remaining 1,600 unsold copies were offered as a "cheap edition." Four years later, the last 800 were sold off as a remainder. The *English Catalogue of Books* lists a "cheap edition" at 5*s* in May 1950.

●

A2d: Vintage (paperback) edition, 1958

MALCOLM LOWRY I UNDER THE VOLCANO I NEW YORK VINTAGE BOOKS 1958

7 5/16 × 4 5/16 inches

[i–iv] [1–2] 3–376 [377–380]

Contents: [i]: half title; [ii]: blank; [iii]: title page; [iv]: copyright; [1]: dedication; [2]: quotes from Sophocles, John Bunyan, and Goethe; 3–[377]: text; [378]: biographic blurb; [379–380]: advertisements.

Binding: Strong yellow (84) paper wrappers lettered in white, red, and black with a triangular red and black volcano design.

Publication: Published February 1958 at $1.25. Production records not available, but went into at least three printings. "First Vintage Edition" on copyright page.

●

A2e: Penguin Modern Classics (paperback) edition, 1962.

MALCOLM LOWRY | (rule) | UNDER | THE VOLCANO | PENGUIN BOOKS | IN ASSOCIATION WITH | JONATHAN CAPE

7 1/8 × 4 3/8 inches

[1–8] 9–46 [47] 48–68 [69] 70–96 [97] 98–152 [153] 154–196 [197] 198–232 [233] 234–254 [255] 256–281 [282] 283–315 [316] 317–336 [337] 338–375 [376–384]

Contents: [1]: descriptive blurb; [2]: blank; [3]: title page; [4]: copyright; [5]: dedication; [6]: blank; [7]: quotes from Sophocles, John Bunyan, and Goethe; [8]: blank; 9–[377]: text; [378]: blank; [379]: "Some recent additions to the Penguin Modern Classics . . ."; [380]: blank; [381–384]: advertisements.

Binding: White paper wrappers printed in black, gray, and orange with a drawing of the Consul and Yvonne on front cover.

Publication. 20,000 copies issued in April 1962 at 5*s*. Reissued in 1963 with a new cover, quantity printed not known. Reprinted as follows: October 1966, 20,000 copies; July 1968, 15,000 copies; November 1969, 15,000 copies; July 1972, 12,500 copies; July 1973, 15,000 copies; September 1974, 15,000 copies; May 1975, 15,000 copies; September 1976, 13,000 copies; July 1977, 13,000 copies; January 1979, 15,000 copies; August 1980, 10,000 copies; October 1981, 10,000 copies. Printings noted on copyright page.

(Continued from front flap)

shot-silk sun-shot medium of infinite flexibility, which can adapt itself to the subtlest shade of perception or mood, or suffuse with the bloodiest of horrors, or vanish upwards in air like the most mystical of rope-tricks."

H. R. Hays (in the *New York Times Book Review*): "It is cause for rejoicing when one encounters a novel which achieves a rich variety of meaning on many levels, which is written in a style both virile and poetic, which possesses profundity of insight, which is, in short, literature. All this applies to *Under the Volcano*, a book which ought to be read by everyone who can be moved by an honest and passionate approach to human experience."

Robert Penn Warren: "Malcolm Lowry has written an ambitious and compelling book. Few novelists I know can create an atmosphere and pace a story as well as he. And at the same time his book has a solid intellectual substructure. *Under the Volcano* is a memorable performance."

Joseph Henry Jackson (in the *San Francisco Chronicle*): "An original work, unlike anything else you have ever read, it possesses power and poetic feeling far and away beyond any novel you'll have seen in years."

J. B. Lippincott Company
Good Books Since 1792
Philadelphia and New York

The story of a novel . . .

Malcolm Lowry began writing *Under the Volcano* in the mid-1930s while living in Cuernavaca, Mexico. In the summer of 1938 he completed a first draft; and by 1941, the year after he and his second wife, Margerie Bonner Lowry, moved to British Columbia, he had finished a second draft, which was turned down by four publishers. "He read their remarks," Mrs. Lowry remembers, "and decided they were right, so he recalled the manuscript from his agent and began another draft of it. Of course, he was also writing poetry, short stories . . . but in the main he concentrated on the *Volcano* and poems."

Under the Volcano was accepted for publication in the spring of 1946. "Malcolm actually rewrote pages of it when he saw it in print," Mrs. Lowry says. "I almost had to tear the proofs from his hands finally to meet publication date, and he was never happy about it."

The novel was published in February, 1947. The first reviews were mixed, but the people who liked it—Conrad Aiken, Robert Penn Warren, Stephen Spender, and Alfred Kazin among others—liked it very much, indeed. Wrote John Woodburn in the *Saturday Review*: "I have never before used the word in a review, and I am aware of the responsibility upon me in using it, but I am of the opinion, carefully considered, that *Under the Volcano* is a work of genius . . . magnificent, tragic, compassionate, and beautiful."

The hard-cover edition of *Under the Volcano* has been out of print for nearly a decade, and its author died in 1957, in England. Nevertheless, Lowry's reputation and that of his book have continued to grow. Between the original publication of *Under the Volcano* and the release of the present edition, two more of Malcolm Lowry's books have been published. *Hear Us O Lord from Heaven Thy Dwelling Place*, a posthumous collection of his short fiction, won Canada's Governor General's Award for Fiction in 1961. *Ultramarine*, Lowry's first novel, published in England more than thirty years ago and revised by the author before his death, was released in the United States for the first time in 1962.

Malcolm LOWRY Under The VOLCANO

Malcolm
LOWRY
introduction by Stephen Spender

Under The
VOLCANO

"*Under the Volcano* has achieved a reputation as one of the few great novels of the century. . . . *Under the Volcano* combines the terror and inevitability of *Moby Dick* with the virtuosity and density of *Ulysses*. Although the book recasts total despair, it plays a counterpoint of ecstasy."

—Conrad Knickerbocker,
New York Times Book Review

MALCOLM

LOWRY

UNDER

THE VOLCANO

With an introduction
by Stephen Spender

This is the story of Geoffrey Firmin—formerly a British consul, but now with no occupation except his fabulous drinking—and of his efforts to rise to the occasion of the unexpected return, in the early morning of The Day of the Dead, of his estranged wife, Yvonne. His half-brother, Hugh, and his boyhood friend, Jacques Laruelle, both of whom are in love with Yvonne, are the other principal actors in this drama of a man's heroic effort to defeat the sinister forces within himself and to seize the opportunities offered him to save himself.

Conrad Aiken: "Malcolm Lowry's *Under the Volcano* must be, for anyone who loves the English language, a sheer joy. Here it is, all renewed and alive again, a changeable

(Continued on back flap)

Jacket design by David Lunn

$5.95

Dust jacket for A2f

A2f: Reissue with Stephen Spender Introduction, 1965

UNDER

THE

VOLCANO

MALCOLM LOWRY

With an Introduction by
Stephen Spender

J. B. LIPPINCOTT COMPANY
PHILADELPHIA AND NEW YORK

1965

A2f: $7\frac{15}{16} \times 5\frac{3}{8}$ inches

Text copyright 1947 by Malcolm Lowry
Introduction copyright © 1965 by J. B. Lippincott Company

PRINTED IN THE UNITED STATES OF AMERICA

Library of Congress Catalog Card Number: *65-11640*

[a–b] [i–vi] vii–xxvi [1–2] 3–375 [376–380]

Contents: [a–b]: blank; [i]: half title; [ii]: "By the Same Author" (three titles); [iii]: title page; [iv]: copyright; [v]: dedication; [vi]: blank; vii–

xxvi: introduction; [1]: second half title; [2]: quotations from Sophocles, John Bunyan, and Goethe; 3–375: text; [376]: blank; [377]: text; [378–380]: blank.

First binding: Light gray (264) paper boards; medium red brown (43) cloth spine lettered in black "UNDER | (squiggle) | THE | VOLCANO | MALCOLM | LOWRY | LIPPINCOTT." White endpapers. Top edge stained red brown to match cloth spine.

Later binding: Deep red (13) paper boards with marbled effect. Black cloth spine lettered in gilt as in first binding. Top edge stained green; fore edge untrimmed. The binding of the second printing is identical to this later binding.

Dust jacket: Coated white paper lettered on front panel in black, with a drawing of a red volcano on a blue background. Back panel and flaps lettered in black and brown on a white background.

Publication: 13,000 copies published 26 January 1965, of which 8,000 were for the Mid-Century Book Club [A2g]. Price $5.95. There was a second printing of 1,500 copies in May 1965 and a third printing of 1,500 copies in December 1980. The second printing is stated on the copyright page, whereas the third printing is indicated by the numeral 3 in the ascending numeral method.

Note: Reproduced photographically from the 1947 Reynal & Hitchcock edition.

●

A2g: Mid-Century Book Club edition, 1965

Bound in medium red brown (43) cloth, spine lettered in black as on trade edition. There is no binder's blind stamp on rear cover. Dust jacket as on trade edition with the exception that the front flap has "053

Book Club Edition" instead of a price and the rear flap drops the publisher's name and adds "Printed in the U.S.A." This edition is slightly taller than the trade edition, measuring 8 3/16 inches. Contents identical to trade edition. 8,000 copies published January 1965.

●

A2h: Signet (paperback) edition, 1966

Under | The | Volcano | by MALCOLM LOWRY | with an introduction by | STEPHEN SPENDER | (publisher's logo) | A SIGNET BOOK | Published by | THE NEW AMERICAN LIBRARY

6 7/8 × 4 1/4 inches

[i–vi] vii–xxvi [xxvii–xxviii] 29–406 [407–408]

Contents: [i]: reviews; [ii]: advertisements for other Signet books; [iii]: title page; [iv]: copyright; [v]: dedication; [vi]: blank; vii–xxvi: introduction; [xxvii]: second half title; [xxviii]: quotations from Sophocles, John Bunyan, and Goethe; 29–406: text; [407–408]: advertisements.

Binding: White paper wrappers lettered in red and black and with a painting of a sun, a volcano, and a figure in yellow, red, black, and green.

Publication: Published in August 1966 at 95¢. Production records not available. First printing stated on copyright page.

Note: This edition omits the last page of the novel, which quotes the sign in the public gardens.

●

A2j: Signet, Canadian (paperback) edition, 1966

Under | The | Volcano | by MALCOLM LOWRY | with an introduction by | STEPHEN SPENDER | (publisher's logo) | A SIGNET BOOK

| Published by | THE NEW AMERICAN LIBRARY | of Canada Limited

6 7/8 × 4 1/4 inches

[i–vi] vii–xxvi [xxvii–xxviii] 29–406 [407–408]

Contents: Identical to the American Signet Edition [A2h].

Binding: Identical to A2h.

Publication: Published in August 1966 at 95¢. Production records not available. First printing stated on copyright page.

Note: This edition also omits the last page of the novel. Printed in Canada; covers printed in the U.S.A.

A2k: Cape edition of reissue with Spender Introduction, 1967

UNDER | THE | VOLCANO | MALCOLM LOWRY | *With an Introduction by* | *Stephen Spender* | (publisher's logo) | JONATHAN CAPE | THIRTY BEDFORD SQUARE | LONDON

7 3/4 × 5 3/16 inches

[i–vi] vii–xxvi [1–2] 3–375 [376–378]

Contents: Identical to the Lippincott edition [A2f] but lacking the first and last blank leaves.

Binding: Purple paper boards lettered horizontally on spine in gilt, "UNDER | THE | VOLCANO | (design) | MALCOLM LOWRY | (publisher's logo)."

Dust jacket: Coated white paper lettered in black and with a design of faces that carries over both panels and spine; flaps lettered in black.

Publication: 3,000 copies published 19 January 1967 at 30*s*. There was a second printing of 1,500 copies in October 1969 and a third of 1,500 copies in October 1975. Printings are indicated on copyright page.

Note: Advance copies in wrappers were issued.

A21: Plume Books (paperback) edition, 1971

MALCOLM LOWRY I UNDER I THE VOLCANO I *With an Introduction by* STEPHEN SPENDER I (publisher's logo) I A PLUME BOOK from I NEW AMERICAN LIBRARY I (rule) I TIMES MIRROR I New York, Toronto and London

7 15/16 × 5 5/16 inches

[i–x] xi–xxx [xxxi–xxxii] [1–2] 3–375 [376–384] (See note.)

Contents: [i]: biographical note; [ii]: blank; [iii]: "By the Same Author" (six titles); [iv]: blank; [v]: title page; [vi]: copyright; [vii]: dedication; [viii]: blank; [ix]: section heading; [x]: blank; xi–xxx: introduction; [xxxi]: half title; [xxxii]: blank; [1]: quotes from Sophocles, John Bunyan, and Goethe; [2]: blank; 3–375: text; [376]: blank; [377]: text; [378–382]: blank; [383–384]: advertisements.

Binding: White paper wrappers lettered in white and gray on a black background on front cover and spine, and with a red flame rising from the 'A' in the word "Volcano" on front cover. Lettered in black on a white ground on back cover.

Publication: Published April 1971 at $3.50. Production records not available, but the book has gone into at least eight printings. First printing noted on copyright page. Later printings are indicated by the ascending numeral method, but the first printing note is retained.

Note: In later printings the front and back matter has been condensed so that the pagination is as follows: [vii–x] xi–xxx [1–2] 3–375 [376].

A3 A LETTER FROM MALCOLM LOWRY

A3: First edition, 1949

A LETTER FROM *Malcolm Lowry* | AUTHOR OF *Under the Volcano* | ABOUT *A Long Day's Dying* | BY *Frederick Buechner*

$8^1/_2 \times 11$ inch sheet folded to make four pages.

Contents: [1–4]: text

Binding: Unbound.

Publication: Neither the publisher, Alfred A. Knopf, nor the author, Frederick Buechner, could supply any information regarding date of publication or number of copies printed. As *A Long Day's Dying* was published early in January 1950, however, and as Lowry's letter was probably written during the first week of November 1949 [see note below], it seems probable that it was issued in November or December 1949.

Note: The letter is quoted on the dust jacket of the book [B7]. The name of the recipient is not given, but in a letter to Albert Erskine dated 7 November 1949 Lowry mentions that "I just wrote something about a very remarkable book sent me by a friend of yours, Mr. Harry Ford, via Knopf." [*Selected Letters,* Lippincott, 1965, p. 184], so it seems likely that the addressee was Ford.

Note: The letter has not been published elsewhere.

Dust jacket for A4a

A4 HEAR US O LORD FROM HEAVEN THY DWELLING PLACE

A4a: First edition, 1961

MALCOLM LOWRY

Hear us
O Lord
from heaven
thy
dwelling place

J. B. LIPPINCOTT COMPANY
PHILADELPHIA AND NEW YORK

A4a: 8 × 5¼ inches

COPYRIGHT © 1961 BY MARGERIE BONNER LOWRY

"Strange Comfort Afforded by the Profession" copyright 1953 by Malcolm Lowry.
"The Bravest Boat" copyright 1954 by Stuart Osborne Lowry.

Some of these stories have appeared in *Partisan Review, The Paris Review, New World Writing 3,* and *New World Writing 18.*

FIRST EDITION

PRINTED IN THE UNITED STATES OF AMERICA

Library of Congress Catalog Card Number 61-8688

[1–12] 13–27 [28] 29–113 [114] 115–173 [174] 175–283 [284–288]

Contents: [1]: blank; [2]: "Also by Malcolm Lowry" (one title); [3]: half title; [4]: blank; [5]: title page; [6]: copyright; [7–8]: publisher's note; [9]:

contents; [10]: blank; [11]: Fishermen's Hymn; [12]: blank; 13–27: The Bravest Boat; [28]: blank; 29–98: Through the Panama; 99–113: Strange Comfort Afforded by the Profession; [114]: blank; 115–173: Elephant and Colosseum; [174]: blank; 175–200: Present Estate of Pompeii; 201–214: Gin and Goldenrod; 215–283: The Forest Path to the Spring; [284–288]: blank.

Binding: Medium blue (182) cloth lettered on top cover "[*light blue*] HEAR US O LORD FROM HEAVEN THY DWELLING PLACE I [*purplish blue*] (emblem)." Lettered horizontally on spine "[*light blue*] HEAR US I O LORD I FROM I HEAVEN I THY I DWELLING I PLACE I [*purplish blue*] (emblem) I [light blue] MALCOLM I LOWRY I LIPPINCOTT." White endpapers.

Dust jacket: Coated white paper lettered in white and light blue on a blue photographic background that extends over front panel and spine. Back panel lettered in black over sheet music which is printed in light blue on a white background. Flaps printed in blue and black on a white background.

Publication: Published 17 April 1961 at $4.95. Production records not available.

Note: Advance copies were issued both in wrappers and bound in the dust jacket.

Note: The publisher's note on pages 7–8 was written by Margerie Lowry. The title was taken from the Manx "Fishermen's Hymn" reproduced on page 11 and on the rear of the dust jacket. Although it was the winner of the Governor General's Award for 1961, the book was not published separately in Canada.

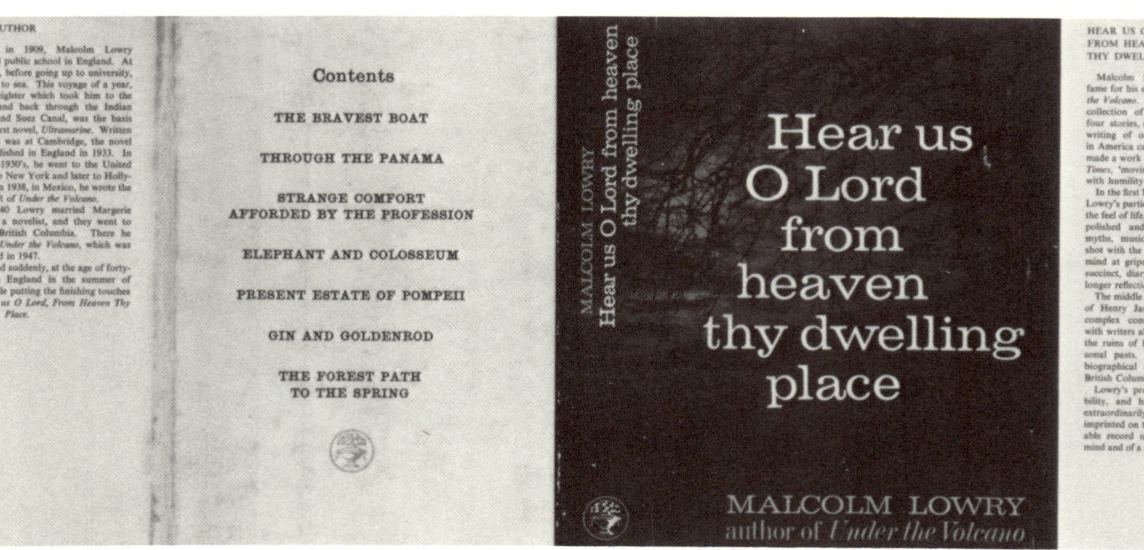

Dust jacket for A4b

A4b: First British edition, 1962

MALCOLM LOWRY

Hear us
O Lord
from heaven
thy
dwelling place

JONATHAN CAPE
30 BEDFORD SQUARE LONDON

A4b: $7\frac{3}{4} \times 5\frac{1}{8}$ inches

FIRST PUBLISHED IN GREAT BRITAIN 1962

COPYRIGHT © 1961 BY MARGERIE BONNER LOWRY

"Strange Comfort Afforded by the Profession" copyright 1953 by Malcolm Lowry.
"The Bravest Boat" copyright 1954 by Stuart Osborne Lowry.

Some of these stories have appeared in *Partisan Review*, *The Paris Review*, *New World Writing 3*, and *New World Writing 18*.

PRINTED BY THE REPLIKA PROCESS IN GREAT BRITAIN
BY PERCY LUND, HUMPHRIES & CO. LTD
LONDON · BRADFORD
BOUND BY A. W. BAIN & CO. LTD, LONDON

[1–12] 13–27 [28] 29–113 [114] 115–173 [174] 175–283 [284–288]. [1–2] and [287–288] serve as free endpapers.

Contents: [1–2]: blank; [3]: half title; [4]: "Also by Malcolm Lowry" (one title); [5]: title page; [6]: copyright; [7–8]: publisher's note; [9]: contents; [10]: blank; [11]: Fishermen's Hymn; [12]: blank; 13–27: The Bravest Boat; [28]: blank; 29–98: Through the Panama; 99–113: Strange Comfort Afforded by the Profession; [114]: blank; 115–173: Elephant and Colosseum; [174]: blank; 175–200: Present Estate of Pompeii; 201–214: Gin and Goldenrod; 215–283: The Forest Path to the Spring; [284–288]: blank.

Binding: Gray blue (186) paper boards lettered horizontally in gilt on spine "MALCOLM I LOWRY I HEAR US I O LORD I FROM I HEAVEN I THY I DWELLING I PLACE I (publisher's logo)."

Dust jacket: Coated white paper lettered in white and light blue on a blue photographic background that extends over front panel and spine. Back panel lettered in black, with the publisher's logo in blue at bottom, on a white background. Flaps lettered in black on a white background.

Publication: 4,000 copies published on 30 April 1962 at 18*s*.

Note: Reproduced by offset from the American edition.

A4c: Keystone Books (paperback) edition, 1963

MALCOLM LOWRY I Hear Us I O Lord I from heaven I thy I dwelling place I J. B. LIPPINCOTT COMPANY I PHILADELPHIA AND NEW YORK

8 × 5 5/16 inches

[1–12] 13–27 [28] 29–113 [114] 115–173 [174] 175–283 [284–288]

Contents: As in the cloth edition (A4a) with the exception that [2] lists three titles by Lowry and [285–286] carry publisher's advertisements.

Binding: White paper wrappers lettered in white and light blue on a blue photographic background (similar to the cloth edition dust jacket) that extends over front cover and spine. Rear cover printed in black and blue on a white ground.

Publication: Published 1963 at $1.95. Production records not available. "First Keystone edition, 1963" on copyright page.

Note: Reproduced by offset from the cloth edition.

A4d: Capricorn (paperback) edition, 1969

MALCOLM LOWRY | Hear us | O Lord | from heaven | thy | dwelling place | Capricorn Books New York

$7^{1}/_{4} \times 4^{1}/_{4}$ inches

[5–12] 13–27 [28] 29–113 [114] 115–173 [174] 175–283 [284–292]

Contents: [5]: half title; [6]: blank; [7]: title page; [8]: copyright; [9–10]: publisher's note; [11]: contents; [12]: Fishermen's Hymn; 13–27: The Bravest Boat; [28]: blank; 29–98: Through the Panama; 99–113: Strange Comfort Afforded by the Profession; [114]: blank; 115–173: Elephant and Colosseum; [174]: blank; 175–200: Present Estate of Pompeii; 201–214: Gin and Goldenrod; 215–283: The Forest Path to the Spring; [284]: blank; [285–289]: publisher's advertisements; [290–292]: blank.

Binding: Paper wrappers lettered in white, red, and yellow on a purple background on front panel and spine. Back cover printed in red and purple on a white background.

Publication: 5,000 copies published 19 May 1969 at $2.25. Out of print on 29 November 1976 and not reprinted.

A4e: Penguin (paperback) edition, 1969

MALCOLM LOWRY | (rule) | Hear us O Lord from Heaven | thy dwelling place | (publisher's logo) | Penguin Books

$7^{1}/_{16} \times 4^{3}/_{8}$ inches

[1–6] 7 [8] 9 [10] 11–97 [98] 99–112 [113] 114–173 [174] 175–200 [201] 202–287 [288]

Contents: [1]: biographical note; [2]: blank; [3]: title page; [4]: copyright; [5]: contents; [6]: blank; 7–[8]: publisher's note; 9: Fishermen's Hymn; [10]: blank; 11–25: The Bravest Boat; 26–[98]: Through the Panama; 99–[113]: Strange Comfort Afforded by the Profession; 114–[174]: Elephant and Colosseum; 175–[201]: Present Estate of Pompeii; 202–215: Gin and Goldenrod; 216–287: The Forest Path to the Spring; [288]: publisher's advertisements.

Binding: White paper wrappers lettered in black and orange on front cover and with a drawing in black of Pompeii. Spine lettered in black and white on an orange background. Back cover lettered in black and orange.

Publication: 20,000 copies published in May 1969 at 30*p*. Not reprinted in this format.

A4f: Penguin Modern Classics (paperback) combined edition, 1979

MALCOLM LOWRY | (rule) | *Hear Us O Lord From Heaven* | *Thy Dwelling Place* | AND | *Lunar Caustic* | (publisher's logo) | PENGUIN BOOKS

7 1/16 × 4 5/16 inches

[i–ii] [1–8] 9 [10] 11–97 [98] 99–112 [113] 114–173 [174] 175–200 [201] 202–287 [288–290] 291 [292] 293 [294] 295–346 [347–350]

Contents: [i]: biographical note; [ii]: blank; [1]: title page; [2]: copyright; [3]: contents; [4]: blank; [5]: half title; [6]: blank; [7–8]: publisher's note; 9: Fishermen's Hymn; [10]: blank; 11–25: The Bravest Boat; 26–[98]: Through the Panama; 99–[113]: Strange Comfort Afforded by the Profession; 114–[174]: Elephant and Colosseum; 175–[201]: Present Estate of Pompeii; 202–215: Gin and Goldenrod; 216–287: The Forest Path to the Spring; [288]: blank; [289]: half title; [290]: blank; 291–[292]: foreword; [293]: note by C(onrad) K(nickerbocker); [294]: blank; 295–346: Lunar Caustic; [347]: publisher's advertisements; [348]: blank; [349–350]: publisher's advertisements.

Binding: Paper wrappers lettered in black on front cover on a background consisting of a painting of equipment on a ship's deck in white, buff, and purple. Spine and back cover lettered in black and white on a green background.

Publication: 10,000 copies published in December 1979 at £1.75.

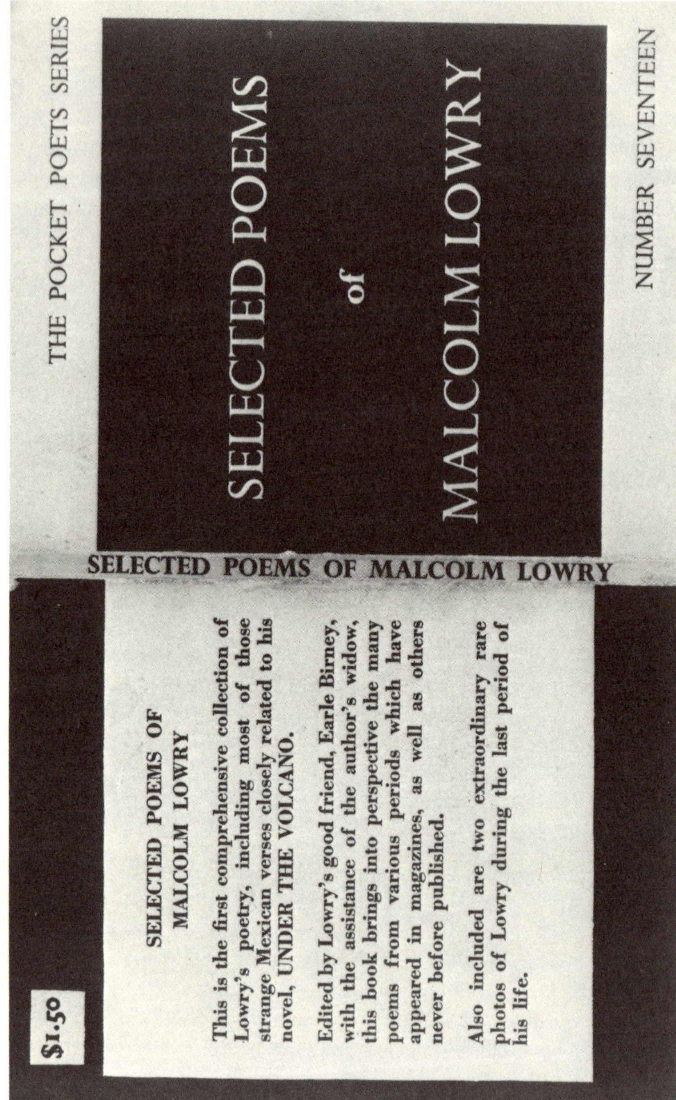

Wrapper for A5

A5 SELECTED POEMS

A5: First edition, 1962

SELECTED POEMS
of
MALCOLM LOWRY

Edited by
EARLE BIRNEY

with the assistance of
Margerie Lowry

CITY LIGHTS BOOKS

A5: $6\frac{3}{16} \times 4\frac{7}{8}$ inches

© 1962 by Margerie Lowry

These poems have been selected and edited from manuscripts at the University of British Columbia. Some of them have already been published, or will appear, in: *Arizona Quarterly, Atlantic Monthly, Audience, Canadian Forum, Canadian Literature, Canadian Poetry Magazine, Contact, Contemporary Verse, Dalhousie Review,. Evidence, Exchange, Fiddlehead, Harpers, Ladies Home Journal, London Magazine, Minnesota Review, New York Times, New Yorker, Northwest Review, Outposts, Paris Review, Perspective, Queens Quarterly, Southwest Review, Tamarack Review, Western Humanities Review, X,* and in A. J. M. Smith's *Book of Canadian Poetry.*

The Pocket Poets Series is published by City Lights Books, 261 Columbus Avenue, San Francisco 11, California, and distributed nationally to bookstores by the Paper Editions Corporation. Overseas distributors: The Scorpion Press, 11 Rofant Road, Northwood, Middlesex, England.

[1–6] 7–79 [80]

Contents: [1]: title page; [2]: copyright; [3]: mariner's proverb; [4–6]: contents; 7–10: Introduction by Earle Birney; 11–79: text; [80]: blank. Photographs inserted between pages [6]–7 and 10–11.

Poems included [section title in italics]: *The Roar of the Sea and the Darkness:* No kraken shall be found till sought by name; Look out! The bloody bosun; Byzantium; Old freighter in an old port; Iron cities; The flowering past; The ship is turning homeward; The lighthouse invites the storm; Tashtego believed red; Vigil Forget; The days like smitten cymbals of brass; *Thunder beyond Popocatepetl:* Thunder beyond Popocatepetl; For *Under the Volcano*; Xochitepec; The volcano is dark; Grim vinegarroon; In the Oaxaca jail; For the love of dying; Death of a Oaxaquenian; In a Mexican church; Delirium in Vera Cruz; Sunrise; *The Cantinas:* Prayer for drunks; Thirty-five mescals in Cuautla; Eye-opener; No company but fear; No time to stop and think; Comfort; Without the nighted wyvern; The drunkards; At the bar; Sestina in a cantina; *Venus:* Venus; Fragment; A new ship; A poem of God's mercy; A quarrel; No still path; Nocturne; Saint Malcolm among the birds; Happiness; Be patient for the wolf; *The Comedian:* The comedian; Men with coats thrashing; Thoughts while drowning; Queer poem; Poem; Midtown pyromaniac; Injured stones; Epitaph: *Songs from the Beach: Eridanus:* Kingfishers in British Columbia; Christ walks in this infernal district too; Whirlpool; Hostage; The glaucous-winged gull; The ship sails on: For Nordahl Grieg; The wounded bat; The past; The pilgrim; The wild cherry; *The Language of Man's Woe:* Rilke and Yeats; Thoughts to be erased from my destiny; Joseph Conrad; Trinity; The doomed in their sinking; Eels; The plagiarist (fragment); He liked the dead; After publication of *Under the Volcano;* The search; Strange type.

Binding: White paper wrappers lettered in black and in white on a black background.

Publication: 1,500 copies published August 1962 at $1.50. Later printings as follows: March 1963, 1,500 copies; March 1964, 1,500 copies; May 1966, 2,500 copies; December 1967, 3,000 copies; December 1969, 3,000 copies; October 1973, 3,000 copies; April 1977, 3,000 copies. First printing not indicated on copyright page but later printings, up to at least the fourth, are indicated on copyright page and back cover. At some time after the fourth printing the printing notice was dropped but these later printings can be distinguished because the covers are of shiny coated stock. They also dropped the "Printed at the Press of Villiers Publications Ltd. Ingestre Road, London, N.W.5, England" at the bottom of page 80.

Note: The second and later printings have four additional photographs (on two leaves) inserted between pages 64–65 and following page [80].

Note: Lowry planned to use the title *The Lighthouse Invites the Storm* for his proposed collection of poems.

Note: An earlier version of "A poem of God's mercy" appeared in B5 under the title "Cain shall not slay Abel today on our good ground."

Note: "The comedian" appears in B5, with slight differences, under the title "He plays the piano with a razor."

Note: An earlier version of "The glaucous-winged gull," without the second line, appears in C40.

Note: The poems "A quarrel" and "Nocturne" appeared in earlier versions under the joint title "Two poems." See C42, C43.

Note: See note to C47 for the transfer of the titles "Lupus in fabula" and "Xochitepec."

Note: The poem "Trinity" was previously published, untitled, in C66.

Note: The poems "The drunkards" and "Without the nighted wyvern" were both originally published in C185 under the joint title "The drunkards."

Note: The poem "A new ship" was originally published, untitled, in C189.

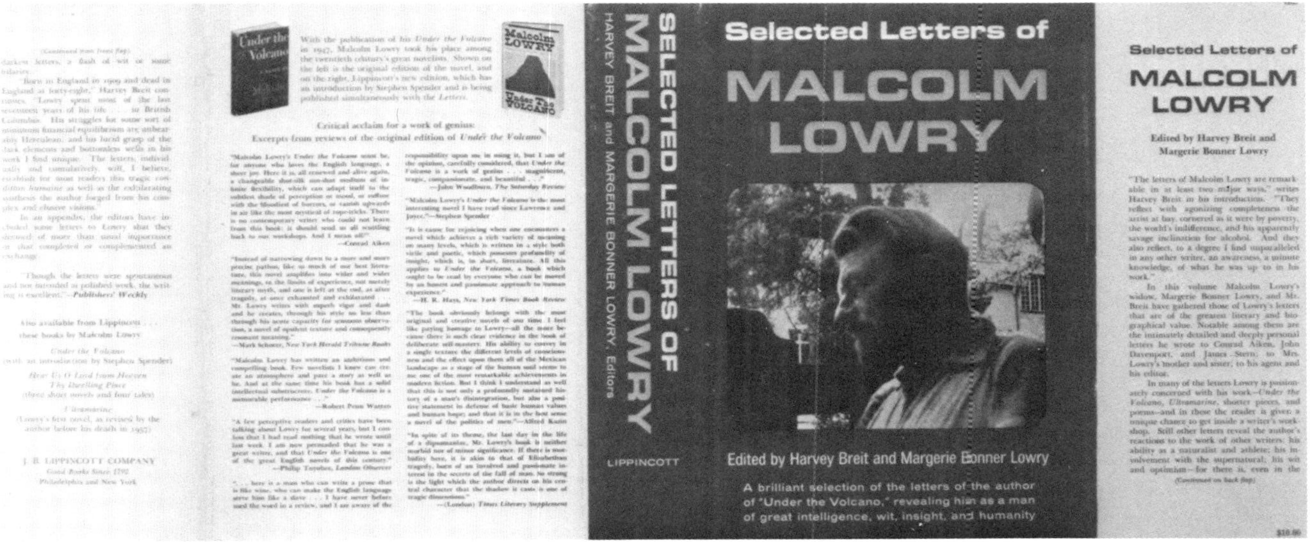

(Continued from front flap)

With the publication of his *Under the Volcano* in 1947, Malcolm Lowry took his place among the twentieth century's great novelists. Shown on the left is the original edition of the novel, and on the right, Lippincott's new edition, which has an introduction by Stephen Spender and is being published simultaneously with the *Letters*.

Critical acclaim for a work of genius:

Excerpts from reviews of the original edition of Under the Volcano

J. B. LIPPINCOTT COMPANY

Good Books Since 1792

Philadelphia and New York

SELECTED LETTERS OF MALCOLM LOWRY

HARVEY BREIT and MARGERIE BONNER LOWRY, Editors

LIPPINCOTT

Selected Letters of

MALCOLM LOWRY

Edited by Harvey Breit and Margerie Bonner Lowry

A brilliant selection of the letters of the author of "Under the Volcano," revealing him as a man of great intelligence, wit, insight, and humanity

Selected Letters of

MALCOLM LOWRY

Edited by Harvey Breit and Margerie Bonner Lowry

"The letters of Malcolm Lowry are remarkable in at least two major ways," writes Harvey Breit in his introduction. "They reflect with agonizing completeness the artist at bay, cornered as it were by poverty, the world's indifference, and his apparently savage inclination for alcohol. And they also reflect, to a degree I find unparalleled in any other writer, an awareness, a minute knowledge, of what he was up to in his work."

In this volume Malcolm Lowry's widow, Margerie Bonner Lowry, and Mr. Breit have gathered those of Lowry's letters that are of the greatest literary and biographical value. Notable among them are the intimately detailed and deeply personal letters he wrote to Conrad Aiken, John Davenport, and James Stern; to Mrs. Lowry's mother and sister; to his agent and his editor.

In many of the letters Lowry is passionately concerned with his work—*Under the Volcano*, *Ultramarine*, shorter pieces, and poems—and in these the reader is given a unique chance to get inside a writer's workshop. Still other letters reveal the author's reactions to the work of other writers; his ability as a naturalist and athlete; his involvement with the supernatural; his wit and optimism—for there is, even in the

(Continued on back flap)

Dust jacket for A6a

A6 SELECTED LETTERS

A6a: First edition, 1965

SELECTED LETTERS OF

Malcolm Lowry

Edited by Harvey Breit & Margerie Bonner Lowry

J. B. LIPPINCOTT COMPANY
Philadelphia & New York

A6a: $8\frac{15}{16} \times 5\frac{15}{16}$ inches

COPYRIGHT © 1965 BY MARGERIE BONNER LOWRY

FIRST EDITION

PRINTED IN THE UNITED STATES OF AMERICA

LIBRARY OF CONGRESS CATALOG CARD NUMBER: 65–11016

Lines from Conrad Aiken's "The House of Dust" are quoted by permission of Oxford University Press, Inc., from Aiken's *Collected Poems,* copyright 1953 by Conrad Aiken.

A passage from José Ortega y Gasset is quoted by permission of W. W. Norton & Company, Inc., from *History as a System, and Other Essays Toward a Philosophy of History,* copyright 1941, © 1961 by W. W. Norton & Company, Inc., New York, N.Y.

Verse LXXVI of "Gitanjali" from *The Collected Poems and Plays of Rabindranath Tagore* is reprinted by permission of The Macmillan Co., the Trustees of the Tagore Estate, and Macmillan & Co., Ltd., London, copyright 1918 by The Macmillan Co., renewed 1946 by Rathindranath Tagore.

[i–viii] ix [x] xi–xv [xvi] xvii–xix [xx] [1–2] 3–34 [35–36] 37–54 [55–56] 57–134 [135–136] 137–160 [161–162] 163–184 [185–186] 187–224 [225–226] 227–281 [282–284] 285–324 [325–326] 327–350 [351–352]

353–376 [377–378] 379–394 [395–396] 397–415 [416–418] 419–453 [454] 455–459 [460]

Contents: [i]: half title; [ii]: blank; [iii]: "Other books by Malcolm Lowry" (three titles); [iv]: blank; [v]: title; [vi]: copyright; [vii]: dedication; [viii]: blank; ix: acknowledgments; [x]: blank; xi–xv: Introduction by Harvey Breit; [xvi]: blank; xvii–xviii: chronology; xix: contents; [xx]: blank; [1]–415: text; [416]: blank; [417]–453: appendixes; [454]: blank; 455–459: index; [460]: blank. Photographic frontispiece tipped in before title page.

Binding: Pale greenish yellow (104) paper boards with a marbled effect; medium yellow green (120) cloth spine lettered horizontally in gilt "(rule) | SELECTED | LETTERS | OF | MALCOLM | LOWRY | (rule) | Edited by | Harvey Breit | & | Margerie | Bonner | Lowry | (rule) | LIPPINCOTT." Green endpapers. Top edge stained green.

Dust jacket: Coated white paper printed in white and yellow on an olive background on front panel and spine, and with a black and white photograph of the author on front panel; back panel and flaps lettered in black on a white ground.

Publication: Published 22 November 1965 at $10.00. Production records not available.

THE AUTHOR

Born in 1909, Malcolm Lowry attended public school in England. At eighteen, before going up to university, he went to sea. This voyage of a year, on a freighter which took him to the Orient and back through the Indian Ocean and the Suez Canal, was the basis for his first novel, *Ultramarine*. Written while he was at Cambridge, the novel was published in England in 1933. In the mid-1930s he went to the United States, to New York and later to Hollywood. In 1938, in Mexico, he wrote the first draft of *Under the Volcano*.

In 1940 Lowry married Margerie Bonner, a novelist, and they went to live in British Columbia. There he rewrote *Under the Volcano*, which was first published in 1947, and is now re-issued with an Introduction by Stephen Spender.

He died suddenly, at the age of forty-eight, in England in the summer of 1957, while putting the finishing touches to *Hear Us O Lord from Heaven Thy Dwelling Place*.

Jacket design by Harry Gordon

Malcolm Lowry
at Tlaxcala, Mexico

THE
SELECTED
LETTERS
OF
MALCOLM
LOWRY

EDITED BY
HARVEY BREIT
& M. B. LOWRY

THE SELECTED LETTERS OF MALCOLM LOWRY

EDITED BY HARVEY BREIT AND MARGERIE BONNER LOWRY

THE SELECTED LETTERS OF MALCOLM LOWRY

The letters of Malcolm Lowry cover his early life in England, his long sojourns first in Mexico and then in British Columbia, the return to Europe and last years in England.

They give a desolating account of the writer's struggle against poverty and indifference and savage addiction to alcohol. They show his deep friendships with other writers and with his editor, and his dependence on his wife. Finally, they reflect the minute awareness of what he was about in his work that makes them a uniquely valuable document for anyone who is interested in the literature of the twentieth century and the impulses that underlie a great work of art.

Dust jacket for A6b

A6b: First British edition, 1967

SELECTED LETTERS OF

Malcolm Lowry

Edited by Harvey Breit & Margerie Bonner Lowry

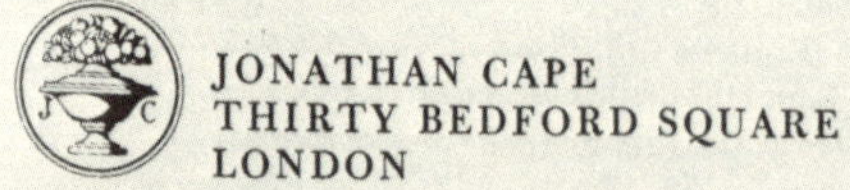

JONATHAN CAPE
THIRTY BEDFORD SQUARE
LONDON

A6b: $8^{3}/_{8} \times 5^{1}/_{2}$ inches

First published in Great Britain 1967

Lines from Conrad Aiken's "The House of Dust" are quoted by permission of Oxford University Press, Inc., from Aiken's *Collected Poems*, copyright 1953 by Conrad Aiken.

A passage from José Ortega y Gasset is quoted by permission of W. W. Norton & Company, Inc., from *History as a System, and Other Essays Toward a Philosophy of History*, copyright 1941, © 1961 by W. W. Norton & Company, Inc., New York, N.Y.

Verse LXXVI of "Gitanjali" from *The Collected Poems and Plays of Rabindranath Tagore* is reprinted by permission of The Macmillan Co., the Trustees of the Tagore Estate, and Macmillan & Co., Ltd., London, copyright 1918 by The Macmillan Co., renewed 1946 by Rathindranath Tagore.

Printed in Great Britain by
Lowe and Brydone (Printers) Ltd, London
on paper made by John Dickinson & Co. Ltd
Bound by A. W. Bain & Co. Ltd, London

Collation and contents as in Lippincott edition (A6a)

Binding: Gray paper boards; purple cloth spine. Lettered horizontally in gilt on spine "THE | SELECTED | LETTERS | OF | MALCOLM | LOWRY | EDITED BY | HARVEY BREIT | & | MARGERIE BONNER LOWRY | (publisher's logo)." White endpapers.

Dust jacket: Coated white paper printed in black. Front panel has a black and white photograph of a Lowry autograph letter; back panel has a black and white photograph of Lowry captioned "Malcolm Lowry at Tlaxcala, Mexico."

Publication: 1,500 copies published on 19 January 1967 at 55*s*. Not reprinted.

Note: Advance copies in wrappers were issued.

●

A6c: Capricorn Books (paperback) edition, 1969

SELECTED LETTERS OF | Malcolm Lowry | *Edited by Harvey Breit & Margerie Bonner Lowry* | Capricorn Books | New York

8 × 5 1/8

Collation and contents as in Lippincott edition (A6a) with the exception that [iii] is blank and [iv] is the frontispiece.

Binding: Paper wrappers lettered on front cover and spine in white, orange, and yellow on a blue background. Back cover lettered in orange and blue on a white background.

Publication: 5,000 copies published 15 May 1969 at $2.95. "CAPRICORN BOOKS EDITION 1969" on copyright page. Out of print on 20 March 1975.

A7 LETTERS BETWEEN MALCOLM LOWRY & JONATHAN CAPE ABOUT "UNDER THE VOLCANO"

A7: First edition, 1966

Letters between Malcolm Lowry & Jonathan Cape about "Under the Volcano"

JONATHAN CAPE
2s 6d net

A7: Front cover. $8^{1/2} \times 5^{1/2}$ inches

[1–36]

Contents: [1]: title page (serving as cover); [2]: publisher's advertisements; [3–35]: text; [36]: "Printed in Great Britain."

Binding: Unbound.

Publication: Production records not available but published late 1966. Some copies have a 2*s*6*d* price sticker at bottom right hand corner of first page.

Note: Issued to promote the Cape edition of *Selected Letters of Malcolm Lowry*, but as noted, copies were also sold.

Dust jacket for A8a

A8 LUNAR CAUSTIC

A8a: First edition, 1968

Lunar Caustic
Malcolm Lowry

Edited by Earle Birney
and Margerie Lowry
With a Foreword by Conrad Knickerbocker

JONATHAN CAPE
THIRTY BEDFORD SQUARE
LONDON

A8a: 7 × 4 1/8 inches

First published in the *Paris Review*, no. 29, 1963
© 1963 by Margerie Lowry
Reissued 1968 by Jonathan Cape Ltd, 30 Bedford Square, London, WC1

The article by Conrad Knickerbocker, 'Malcolm Lowry and the Outer Circle of Hell', is reprinted by permission of Russell & Volkening Inc.

SBN Paperback edition 224 61340 5
Hardbound edition 224 61339 1

Condition of Sale

This book is sold subject to the condition that it shall not, by way of trade or otherwise, be lent, re-sold, hired out, or otherwise circulated without the publisher's prior consent in any form of binding or cover other than that in which it is published and without a similiar condition being imposed on the subsequent purchaser.

Printed and bound in Great Britain
by Richard Clay (The Chaucer Press), Ltd
Bungay, Suffolk

[1–4] 5–7 [8] 9–78 [79–80]

Contents: [1]: "CAPE EDITIONS 13"; [2]: blank; [3]: title page; [4]: copyright; 5–7: "*Malcolm Lowry and the Outer Circle of Hell*" by Conrad Knickerbocker; [8]: note by C(onrad) K(nickerbocker); 9–76: text; 77:

biographical note; 78: "SÉLECTED BIBLIOGRAPHY"; [79–80]: blank.

Binding: Black paper boards lettered in silver up spine "Lunar Caustic Malcolm Lowry," with publisher's logo at base of spine. White endpapers.

Dust jacket: Front and back panels printed in white and dark green on a light green background; spine and flaps lettered in dark green on a light green background.

Publication: 1,500 copies published at 16*s* on 22 February 1968 but see A8b. A second printing of 500 copies was issued in 1971. Reissued 1977 (see A8c).

Note: The printing history of *Lunar Caustic* is complicated. Douglas Day, in his biography of Lowry (Oxford University Press, 1973) p. 197 et seq., explains how it was written. The first version was a short story, "The Last Address," written in New York shortly after Lowry's discharge from Bellevue Hospital in June 1935. [According to Day this short story version was lost and has never been found.] Lowry then, in New York and California in 1935/36, revised and expanded this version into a novella, still using "The Last Address" as the title. This was declined by Lowry's agent, Harold Matson, and Lowry then began another version. This was called "Swinging the Maelstrom," and was written in Mexico and British Columbia. Lowry then put this version away but in the last months of his life he made a thorough revision under the title "Lunar Caustic."

In 1948, when Lowry was in Paris, he gave Clarisse Francillon a copy of the typescript of "Swinging the Maelstrom" and she, with Michele d'Astorg, translated it and it was published serially in *Esprit*, Paris, February, March, and April 1956 (D21).

The first printing in English came in 1963 when the *Paris Review* in its Winter/Spring issue (C199) published the version put together by Margerie Lowry and Earle Birney from the three different versions that were found after Lowry's death. This English version was then, again, translated by Clarisse Francillon and published as the complete issue of *Les lettres nouvelles*, Paris, April 1963 (D24).

The *Paris Review* version was then given its first book publication by Cape (A8a) in 1968. The first American publication was in *Malcolm Lowry: Psalms and Songs,* New American Library, 1975 (B18). Then in

1977, both French versions were published in one volume by *Les lettres nouvelles*/Maurice Nadeau (D17).

A8b: Cape (paperback) edition, 1968

4,500 sets of sheets of the first edition were bound in stiff white paper wrappers lettered in gray on top cover "*Lunar* | *Caustic* | *Malcolm* | *Lowry* | CAPE EDITIONS," and up spine "Lunar Caustic Malcolm Lowry." These were issued in trimmed dust jackets of the first edition. Published simultaneously with the hardcover edition, they were priced at 7*s*6*d*. Pagination and contents are identical to the hardcover edition. There was a second printing of 1,500 copies of the paperback edition in July 1968.

A8c: Cape reissue, 1977

[1–5] 6–7 [8] 9–76 [77–78]

Contents: [1]: half title; [2]: "by the same author" (six titles); [3]: title page; [4]: copyright; [5]–7: "*Malcolm Lowry and the Outer Circle of Hell*" by Conrad Knickerbocker; [8]: note by C(onrad) K(nickerbocker); 9–76: text; [77–78]: blank and serving as rear free endpaper.

Binding: Gray blue (186) paper boards lettered down spine in gilt "LUNAR CAUSTIC *Malcolm Lowry* (publisher's logo)." White endpapers (see above).

Dust jacket: Coated white paper lettered in blue and black on front panel and spine and with a drawing in blue and black of a human head and moons extending over both panels and spine. Flaps lettered in black.

Publication: 2,000 copies published 3 March 1977 at £2.50. "Reissued 1977 in this format" on copyright page.

Note: The Penguin Modern Classics edition of *Lunar Caustic/Hear Us O Lord From Heaven Thy Dwelling Place* is listed under A4f.

(*Continued from front flap*)

"The facts of the Lowrys' journey to Mexico in 1945–46 are only the bare bones of *Dark As the Grave*. Lowry was nothing if not a symbolizer: whatever happened, whatever he heard or saw, had to *mean* something, however obliquely.... Thus Sigbjørn Wilderness is not simply Malcolm Lowry taking his wife on a vacation to Mexico: he is a Dante or a Virgil on his way down into the Inferno. And more than they, because he is going back a second time. And the hell is no one else's but his own....

"Now, this book is no *Under the Volcano*. It might have been but it isn't. There are too many loose ends, too many undeveloped ideas, too many images of intended great significance which never seem more than vaguely portentous....

"*Dark As the Grave Wherein My Friend Is Laid* is a work of embryonic greatness. We can lament its imperfect state, but we can also be glad to have it even as it is.' Sigbjørn Wilderness, like his creator, was a man worth knowing."

Malcolm Lowry was born in England in 1909 and attended public school in that country. At eighteen, before going to Cambridge, Lowry went to sea. That voyage of a year, on a freighter to the Orient and back through the Indian Ocean and the Suez Canal, was used as background material for his first novel, *Ultramarine*, which was written while he was at Cambridge and published in England in 1933.

During the nineteen-thirties, Lowry came to the United States, living in New York and Hollywood. In 1938, he went to Mexico and wrote the first draft of *Under the Volcano*. In 1940, Lowry married Margerie Bonner (also a novelist) and they lived much of their life together in British Columbia, Canada. At Dollarton, near Vancouver, Lowry rewrote *Under the Volcano*, which was published in 1947. *Hear Us O Lord from Thy Dwelling Place* was written for the most part in British Columbia, between 1950 and 1954. *Dark As the Grave Wherein My Friend Is Laid* reflects a catastrophic trip the Lowrys made to Mexico in the winter of 1945–6. Malcolm Lowry died suddenly in England in 1957.

Jacket Design: Paul Bacon

NAL

THE NEW AMERICAN LIBRARY

1301 AVENUE OF THE AMERICAS, NEW YORK, N.Y. 10019

PUBLISHERS OF SIGNET, SIGNET CLASSICS, AND MENTOR BOOKS

Malcolm Lowry

DARK AS THE GRAVE WHEREIN MY FRIEND IS LAID

UNDER THE VOLCANO

DARK AS THE GRAVE WHEREIN MY FRIEND IS LAID

Malcolm Lowry

DARK AS THE GRAVE WHEREIN MY FRIEND IS LAID

UNDER THE VOLCANO

$5.95

About *Dark As the Grave Wherein My Friend Is Laid* Douglas Day, Malcolm Lowry's biographer, writes: "In early December, 1945, Malcolm and Margerie Bonner Lowry flew from Vancouver, British Columbia, to Mexico City. They traveled by bus down to Cuernavaca, where Lowry had lived with his first wife, Jan, in 1936, and where he had begun *Under the Volcano*. On New Year's Eve Lowry heard from Jonathan Cape, to whom the completed manuscript of *Under the Volcano* had been sent, that they could not accept the novel as it stood; many revisions were needed. For the next two weeks Lowry spent most of his time writing one of the most remarkable literary documents of our time: a letter to Cape, in which he dissected and analyzed every chapter of *Under the Volcano*, explaining why every detail had to be left as it was. This task was hardly impeded by the events of the night of January 10, when Lowry made a half-hearted and spontaneously conceived attempt to slash his wrists. On January 16 the two set out for Oaxaca, where Lowry hoped to find a Mexican friend from his first stay in that country. They discovered that the man had been dead for some years; and, their reason for being in Oaxaca being nonexistent, they left for Acapulco via Mexico City the following day.

"This much is the matter of *Dark As the Grave Wherein My Friend Is Laid*. During the entire trip both Lowry and his wife made notes as they went along—dialogues, descriptions, copies of signs along the way, all sorts of random observations. After a series of dreadful comic catastrophies in Acapulco and Mexico City, which culminated in their deportation from the country (and about which Lowry wrote yet another unfinished novel, *La Mordida*), they returned to Canada. Some short time afterwards, Lowry looked through all the notes of the Mexican journey, exclaimed, 'By God, we have a novel here!' and fell to work on *Dark As the Grave*."

Seven hundred pages of notes and drafts were left by Lowry in 1952 and not returned to before his death in 1957. These seven hundred pages have been edited to form the present volume by Malcolm Lowry's widow, Margerie Bonner Lowry, and his biographer, Douglas Day.

(*Continued on back flap*)

Dust jacket for A9a

A9 DARK AS THE GRAVE WHEREIN MY FRIEND IS LAID

A9a: First edition, 1968

DARK AS THE GRAVE

WHEREIN

BY

MALCOLM LOWRY

MY FRIEND

EDITED BY

Douglas Day & Margerie Lowry

IS LAID

NAL

The New American Library

A9a: $8\frac{5}{16} \times 5\frac{1}{2}$ inches

[i–viii] ix–xxiii [xxiv–xxvi] 1–17 [18] 19–93 [94] 95–111 [112] 113–131 [132] 133–159 [160] 161–205 [206] 207–255 [256–262]

Contents: [i–iii]: blank; [iv]: half title (running through to [v]) and "Books by Malcolm Lowry" (five titles listed); [v]: continuation of half title; [vi–vii]: double title page; [viii]: copyright; ix–xxiii: Preface by Douglas Day; [xxiv–xxv]: second half title; [xxvi]: blank; 1–255: text; [256]: blank; [257]: "About the author"; [258–262]: blank.

Copyright © 1968 by Margerie Bonner Lowry
Preface Copyright © 1968 by Douglas Day
All rights reserved.
No part of this book may be reproduced without
the written permission of the publishers.
First Printing
Published by The New American Library, Inc.
1301 Avenue of the Americas, New York, New York 10019
Published simultaneously in Canada by
General Publishing Company, Ltd.
Library of Congress Catalog Card Number: 68–26029
Printed in the United States of America

Binding: Black cloth lettered horizontally on spine "[*red*] DARK | (brown rule) | [*red*] AS THE GRAVE | (brown rule) | [*red*] WHEREIN |

(brown rule) | [*red*] MY FRIEND | (brown rule) | [*red*] IS LAID | (brown rule) | [*yellow*] MALCOLM | (brown rule) | [*yellow*] LOWRY | (brown rule) | [*red*] NAL." "H0156" is stamped in red on back cover. Red endpapers. Fore edge untrimmed.

Dust jacket: Coated paper; panels and spine lettered in white and yellow on a black background; red rules and yellow Aztec heads on front and back panels. Publisher's logo in red at base of spine. Flaps lettered in black and red on a white ground.

Publication: Published August 1968 at $5.95. There was a second printing the same year. Production records not available.

Note: Advance copies in wrappers and also in the dust jacket were issued for in-house and review purposes.

Note: Tony Bareham notes in the *Malcolm Lowry Newsletter* #1 that the title is taken from the last stanza of Abraham Cowley's poem "On the Death of Mr. William Hervey."

> Henceforth, ye gentle trees, forever fade;
> Or your sad branches thicker join,
> And into darksome shades combine
> Dark as the grave wherein my friend is laid.

A9b: Canadian edition, 1968

New American Library exported jacketed copies to General Publishing Co., Ltd., Toronto. They are identical to the NAL copies with the exception that the name of the Canadian publisher appears on the title page and at the bottom of the spine of both the book and the dust jacket. Name of American publisher is also deleted from back flap of the dust jacket. Number of copies not known.

Dust jacket for A9c

A9c: First British edition, 1969

MALCOLM LOWRY

DARK AS THE GRAVE
WHEREIN MY FRIEND
IS LAID

EDITED BY
DOUGLAS DAY
AND
MARGERIE LOWRY

JONATHAN CAPE
THIRTY BEDFORD SQUARE
LONDON

A9c: 7 3/4 × 5 1/4 inches

FIRST PUBLISHED IN GREAT BRITAIN 1969

JONATHAN CAPE LTD,
30 BEDFORD SQUARE, LONDON WC1

SBN 224 61656 0

PRINTED IN GREAT BRITAIN BY
LOWE AND BRYDONE (PRINTERS) LIMITED, LONDON
ON PAPER MADE BY JOHN DICKINSON & CO. LTD
BOUND BY A. W. BAIN & CO. LTD, LONDON

[a–b] [i–iv] v–xviii [xix–xx] 1–17 [18] 19–93 [94] 95–111 [112] 113–131 [132] 133–159 [160] 161–205 [206] 207–255 [256–258]. First and last leaves serve as free endpapers.

Contents: [a–b]: free endpaper; [i]: half title; [ii]: "by the same author" (four titles); [iii]: title page; [iv]: copyright; v–xviii: Preface by Douglas Day; [xix]: second half title; [xx]: blank; 1–255: text; [256]: blank; [257–258]: free endpaper.

Binding: Black paper boards lettered up spine in gilt "Dark as the grave wherein my friend is laid   Malcolm Lowry" and with publisher's logo at base of spine. White endpapers. Top edge stained purple.

Dust jacket: Coated white paper lettered in purple and black and with a design of faces and cacti in black running over both panels and spine. Flaps lettered in black.

Publication: 3,000 copies published on 26 June 1969 at 35*s.* There was a second printing of 2,000 copies in August 1969.

Note: Advance copies in wrappers were issued.

A9d: Meridian Books (paperback) edition, 1969

Double title page layout identical to New American Library edition (A9a) with the exception of imprint "MERIDIAN BOOKS | The World Publishing Company | NEW YORK AND CLEVELAND."

$7\frac{15}{16} \times 5\frac{1}{4}$ inches

Pagination and contents same as New American Library edition.

Binding: Coated white paper wrappers lettered on front cover in black and red and with a drawing in yellow and black of an Aztec head. Spine lettered in black and yellow; back cover lettered in red and black.

Publication: Published 1969 at $2.95. Production details not available.

Note: First printing stated on copyright page.

A9e: Penguin Modern Classics (paperback) edition, 1972

MALCOLM LOWRY | (rule) | DARK AS THE GRAVE | WHEREIN | MY FRIEND IS LAID | *Edited by Douglas Day* | *and* | *Margerie Lowry* | (publisher's logo) | PENGUIN BOOKS

7 1/16 × 4 5/16 inches

[1–4] 5–34 [35] 36–64 [65] 66–86 [87] 88–109 [110] 111–126 [127] 128–145 [146] 147–171 [172] 173–202 [203] 204–217 [218] 219–253 [254] 255–266 [267–272]

Contents: [1]: biographical note; [2]: blank; [3]: title page; [4]: copyright; 5–18: Preface by Douglas Day; 19–[267]: text; [268]: blank; [269]: publisher's advertisements; [270]: blank; [271–272]: publisher's advertisements.

Binding: Paper wrappers lettered in white on front cover on a background painting in greens, blues, and white of a tree with cabinet openings holding a sphere and a model of a house; spine and back cover lettered in black and white on a green background.

Publication: 15,000 copies published in January 1972 at 40*p*. Reprinted 13,000 copies in July 1975 and 15,000 copies in August 1979. Printings noted on copyright page.

Note: Advance copies in wrappers were issued.

A10 THE WANDERING JEW

A10: First edition, 1970

A10: Front cover. 8¼ × 5$^{7}/_{16}$ inches

[i–ii] 1–7 [8] [no 9–90] 91–109 [110–112]

Contents: [i]: "To my friends at the ABA"; [ii]: blank; [1]: publisher's advertisement for *October Ferry to Gabriola*; [2]: blank; [3]: letter from James Wade, Senior Editor of World (Publishing) to Peter Matson; [4]: blank; 5–7: "From the wife of Malcolm Lowry"; [8]: blank; 91–109: text; [110–112]: blank.

Binding: Medium yellow green (120) paper wrappers lettered in green on a black rectangular background "*Malcolm* | *Lowry's* | *LAST NOVEL* | *October* | *Ferry to* | *Gabriola*" and with the port and starboard lights on each side of the third line. The cover reproduces in black and green the front panel of the dust jacket of the published book.

Publication: Published in 1970 as a giveaway at the American Booksellers' Association convention in Washington, D.C., 7–10 June 1970. Production records not available.

Note: Contains chapter 20, "The Wandering Jew," from *October Ferry to Gabriola*, but the pagination does not match that in the published book. "From the wife of Malcolm Lowry" becomes an afterword ("Editor's note") in the published book. There are some insignificant differences between the two texts but the only one of any importance corrects the title of D. H. Lawrence's *Aspects of American Literature* (p. 97 in *The Wandering Jew*) to *Studies in Classic American Literature* (p. 137 in *October Ferry to Gabriola*).

Dust jacket for A11a

A11 OCTOBER FERRY TO GABRIOLA

A11a: First edition, 1970

October Ferry
to Gabriola

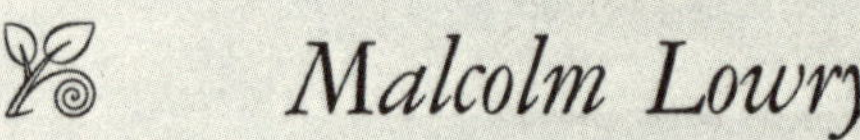
Malcolm Lowry

EDITED BY MARGERIE LOWRY

THE WORLD PUBLISHING COMPANY
New York and Cleveland

A11a: $8^{1}/_{4} \times 5^{1}/_{2}$ inches

Published by The World Publishing Company
Published simultaneously in Canada
by Nelson, Foster & Scott Ltd.
First printing—1970
Copyright © 1970 by Margerie Bonner Lowry
All rights reserved
Library of Congress catalog card number: 70–128492
Printed in the United States of America
Designed by Jacqueline Schuman

WORLD PUBLISHING
TIMES MIRROR

[i–xii] [1–2] 3–333 [334] 335–338 [339–340]

Contents: [i]: half title; [ii]: blank; [iii]: "Books by Malcolm Lowry" (seven titles); [iv]: blank; [v]: title page; [vi]: copyright; [vii–viii]: contents; [ix]: quotes from George Eliot and Chaucer; [x]: blank; [xi]: dedication; [xii]: blank; [1]: second half title; [2]: blank; 3–333: text; [334]: blank; 335–336: "Editor's Note" signed by Margerie Lowry; 337–338: "About the Author"; [339–340]: blank.

Binding: Vivid reddish orange (34) cloth lettered down spine in gilt "*Malcolm Lowry* (ornament) October Ferry | to Gabriola" and with publisher's logo at bottom of spine. White endpapers. Fore edge untrimmed.

Dust jacket: Coated paper lettered in white on a black background and with red and green port and starboard ship's lights on front panel. Spine and back panel lettered in white on a green background and with a black and white photograph of the author on back panel. Front flap lettered in black and green on a white ground and rear flap lettered in black, green, and red on a white ground.

Publication: Published in October 1970 at $6.95. There was a second printing in November 1970. Production records not available.

Note: Advance copies in wrappers were issued.

Note: The plastic coating on the dust jacket of the first printing was faulty, which resulted in crinkling on most copies.

Dust jacket for A11b

A11b: First British edition, 1971

October Ferry to Gabriola

Malcolm Lowry

EDITED BY MARGERIE LOWRY

JONATHAN CAPE
THIRTY BEDFORD SQUARE LONDON

A11b: $7\frac{3}{4} \times 4\frac{15}{16}$ inches

FIRST PUBLISHED IN GREAT BRITAIN 1971

JONATHAN CAPE LTD., 30 BEDFORD SQUARE, LONDON WC1

ISBN 0 224 00532 4

THE PUBLISHERS ARE GRATEFUL TO PETER OWEN LTD. FOR PERMISSION TO QUOTE FROM *Demian* BY HERMAN HESSE, TRANSLATED BY W. J. STRACHAN.

PRINTED IN GREAT BRITAIN
BY LOWE AND BRYDONE (PRINTERS) LTD, LONDON
BOUND BY G. AND J. KITCAT LTD, LONDON

[i–xii] [1–2] 3–333 [334] 335–336 [337–340]

Contents: [i–iv]: blank; [v]: half title; [vi]: "by the same author" (six titles);

[vii]: title page; [viii]: copyright; [ix–x]: contents; [xi]: dedication; [xii]: quotes from George Eliot and Chaucer; [1]: second half title; [2]: blank; 3–333: text; [334]: blank; [335–336]: "Editor's Note" signed by Margerie Lowry; [337–340]: blank.

Binding: Dark red (16) paper boards lettered horizontally on spine in gilt "OCTOBER I FERRY I TO I GABRIOLA I (ornament) I MALCOLM I LOWRY I (publisher's logo)." White endpapers. Top edge stained light blue.

Dust jacket: Coated white paper lettered in black and olive and with a design of faces in black running over both panels and spine. Flaps lettered in black.

Publication: 3,500 copies published 26 August 1971 at £2.25.

Note: Advance copies in proof dust jacket were issued.

A11c: Plume Books (paperback) edition, 1971

October Ferry I to Gabriola (ornament) I (ornament) *Malcolm Lowry* I *EDITED BY MARGERIE LOWRY* I (publisher's logo) I A PLUME BOOK from I NEW AMERICAN LIBRARY I (rule) I TIMES MIRROR I New York, London, and Scarborough, Ontario

8 × 5$^3/_8$ inches

[i–xii] [1–2] 3–333 [334] 335–338 [339–340]

Contents: [i]: biographical note; [ii]: blank; [iii]: half title; [iv]: blank; [v]: "Books by Malcolm Lowry" (seven titles); [vi]: blank; [vii]: title page; [viii]: copyright; [ix–x]: contents; [xi]: quotes from George Eliot and Chaucer; [xii]: blank; [1]: dedication; [2]: blank; 3–333: text; [334]: blank; 335–336: "Editor's Note" signed by Margerie Lowry; 337–338: "About the Author"; [339–340]: blank.

Binding: Coated paper wrappers lettered in yellow, white, and black with a stylistic wave in black and white, all on a brown background. Spine lettered in black on a brown background; back cover lettered in black on a white ground.

Publication: Published December 1971 at $3.50. Production records not available. "First PLUME Printing, December 1971" on copyright page. Has gone into a second printing in which the first printing notice has not been removed, but the ascending numeral method has been added which indicates a second printing. The price of this later printing has been raised to $3.95.

A11d: Penguin Modern Classics (paperback) edition, 1979

MALCOLM LOWRY | OCTOBER FERRY | TO GABRIOLA | *Edited by Margerie Lowry* | (publisher's logo) | PENGUIN BOOKS

7 1/16 × 4 3/8 inches

[1–5] 6 [7–9] 10–11 [12] 13–15 [16] 17 [18] 19–22 [23] 24–28 [29] 30–35 [36] 37–43 [44] 45–50 [51] 52–54 [55] 56–64 [65] 66–70 [71] 72–78 [79] 80–84 [85] 86–94 [95] 96–103 [104] 105–112 [113] 114–115 [116] 117–124 [125] 126–131 [132] 133–150 [151–152] 153–163 [164] 165–172 [173] 174–180 [181] 182–189 [190] 191–204 [205] 206–216 [217] 218–231 [232] 233–244 [245] 246–252 [253] 254–269 [270] 271–282 [283] 284–291 [292] 293–300 [301] 302–308 [309] 310–319 [320] 321–329 [330–331] 332 [333–336]

Contents: [1]: biographical note; [2]: blank; [3]: title page; [4]: copyright; [5]–6: contents; [7]: dedication; [8]: quotes from George Eliot and Chaucer; [9]–329: text; [330]: blank; [331]–332: "Editor's Note" signed by Margerie Lowry; [333]: publisher's advertisements; [334]: blank; [335 336]: publisher's advertisements.

Binding: Coated paper wrappers lettered in white on front cover on a background of a multicolored painting of a view from the stern of a ship. Spine and back cover lettered in black and white on a green background.

Publication: 15,000 copies published in August 1979 at £1.50. "Published in Penguin Books 1979" on copyright page.

A12 CHINA and KRISTBJORG'S STORY IN THE BLACK HILLS

A12: First edition, 1974

MALCOLM LOWRY

CHINA

AND

KRISTBJORG'S STORY IN THE BLACK HILLS

ALOE EDITIONS 1974

A12: $9\frac{1}{4} \times 5\frac{5}{8}$ inches

[1–20]

Contents: [1–2]: blank; [3]: title page; [4]: copyright; [5–12]: "China"; [13–16]: "Kristbjorg's Story"; [17]: "This edition, designed & printed by Ronald Gordon at The Oliphant Press, New York, consists of 150 numbered copies (number written in ink)"; [18–20]: blank.

Binding: Dark greenish yellow (103) paper wrappers with fold over flaps lettered in black on front cover "*CHINA* | *AND* | *KRISTBJORG'S STORY IN THE* | *BLACK HILLS*." Fore edge untrimmed.

Publication: 150 copies published 1 March 1974 at $15.00. The publisher states that there were no advance copies and no overrun.

Note: A short excerpt from "China" was previously published in Tony Kilgallin's *Lowry* (B16). Both stories were collected in *Malcolm Lowry: Psalms and Songs* (B18).

Dust jacket for A13

A13 NOTES ON A SCREENPLAY FOR F. SCOTT FITZGERALD'S TENDER IS THE NIGHT

A13: First edition, 1976

MALCOLM LOWRY
MARGERIE BONNER LOWRY

Notes on a Screenplay for
F. Scott Fitzgerald's
TENDER IS THE NIGHT

Introduction by Paul Tiessen

Bruccoli Clark
Bloomfield Hills, Michigan
Columbia, South Carolina
1976

A13: 9 × 5 3/4 inches

[i–v] vi–xix [xx–xxii] [1] 2–5 [6] 7–84 [85–86]

Contents: [i]: half title; [ii]: blank; [iii]: title page; [iv]: copyright; [v]–xix: introduction; [xx]: blank; [xxi]: second half title; [xxii]: blank; [1]–81:

text, with "Editorial Notes" signed M(atthew) J. B(ruccoli) on p. 81; 82–84: notes; [85–86]: blank.

Binding: Deep reddish orange (36) cloth lettered down spine in gilt "LOWRY" and with publisher's logo at base of spine. White endpapers.

Dust jacket: Coated paper lettered in black on front panel on a background photograph of Fitzgerald in pinkish tones. Spine lettered in white on a reddish orange background that extends over the back panel. Flaps lettered in black on a white ground.

Publication: 300 plus 27 overrun copies published 1 February 1976 at $30.00. The overrun copies were used for review and are so marked. The limitation is stated on rear flap of dust jacket.

Note: Paul Tiessen's introduction quotes from a number of unpublished letters from Lowry to Frank Taylor.

Note: Written together with Margerie Bonner Lowry.

SECTION B
Contributions
to
Books

B. Contributions to Books

B1 CAMBRIDGE POETRY 1930

CAMBRIDGE POETRY | 1930 | EDITED BY | JOHN DAVENPORT | HUGH SYKES & MICHAEL REDGRAVE | (publisher's logo) | Published by Leonard & Virginia Woolf at The | Hogarth Press, 52 Tavistock Square, London, W.C.1 | 1930

[1]–[72]. $7^{3}/_{16} \times 4^{3}/_{4}$ inches. Pinkish tan paper boards printed in black on front cover and up spine. White endpapers. Issued without dust jacket.

Published May 1930 at 3*s*6*d*; 800 copies, of which 300 were later pulped.

Contains the poem "For Nordahl Grieg ship's fireman," 47–49.

B2 THE BEST BRITISH SHORT STORIES OF 1931 1931

THE BEST | BRITISH SHORT STORIES | OF 1931 | EDITED BY | EDWARD J. O'BRIEN | (publisher's logo) | DODD, MEAD & COMPANY | NEW YORK 1931

[i]–xii [1]–324. $7^{11}/_{16} \times 5^{1}/_{4}$ inches. Dark blue cloth, white paper labels printed in blue on front cover and spine. White endpapers. Fore edge untrimmed. Dust jacket not seen.

Published November 1931 at $2.50. Production records not available. First printing not stated on copyright page.

Contains the short story "Seductio Ad Absurdum," 80–107.

Note: Reprinted from *Experiment*, Spring 1931 (C30), where it appeared under the title "Punctum Indifferens Skibet Gaar Videre." There are minor differences between the two versions ("flourish of trumpets" becomes "flourish of strumpets") and the O'Brien version adds several lines on last few pages. Later rewritten and considerably added to and used as chapter IV of *Ultramarine.*

Note: Published in England as *Best Stories of 1931. I: English* (Jonathan Cape, 1932).

B3 I BRING NOT PEACE 1932

I BRING NOT PEACE I By I CHARLOTTE HALDANE I 1932 I CHATTO & WINDUS I LONDON

[i–viii] 1–[316]. 7$^{3}/_{8}$ × 4$^{5}/_{8}$ inches. Medium blue cloth lettered horizontally in gilt on spine. White endpapers. Top edge stained blue; bottom edge untrimmed. White dust jacket printed in black.

Published 5 May 1932 at 7*s*6*d*. 1,500 copies published. First printing not stated on copyright page.

Contains untitled song lyrics by Lowry, "here is all the music that's within my soul," 69; "Give me the money," 262; "And when I die it'll be just the same," 262; and "Rich man, poor man, beggarman, thief," 263.

Note: The book is dedicated to Lowry, and the character James Dowd has many similarities to the Malcolm Lowry of that period.

B4 MASTERS OF THE DEW 1947

Masters of the Dew I *By JACQUES ROUMAIN* I TRANSLATED BY I LANGSTON HUGHES I AND MERCER COOK I *Reynal & Hitchcock New York*

[i–xii] 1–180. 8 × 5$^{1}/_{4}$ inches. Gray cloth lettered down spine in red. White endpapers. White dust jacket lettered in white against a purplish red background on front panel and lettered in purplish red on spine, back panel, and flaps.

Published June 1947 at $3.50. Production records not available. First printing not stated on copyright page.

Contains a nineteen-line blurb by Lowry on back panel of dust jacket.

Note: Copies were issued with the Liberty Book Club imprint at base of spine of book and dust jacket.

B5 A BOOK OF CANADIAN POETRY 1948
Second revised edition

A CRITICAL AND HISTORICAL ANTHOLOGY | *The Book of* | Canadian Poetry | EDITED WITH AN INTRODUCTION AND NOTES BY | A.J.M. SMITH | REVISED EDITION | (publisher's logo) | THE UNIVERSITY OF CHICAGO PRESS . CHICAGO | *In Canada:* W.J. GAGE & CO., LIMITED, TORONTO

[i]–xxiv [1]–[488]. 9×5⅞ inches. Brown cloth lettered horizontally in gilt on a red background at top of spine and in gilt at bottom of spine. White endpapers. Buff dust jacket printed in blue/gray.

3,546 copies published 16 August 1948 at $5.00. Second edition stated on copyright page. Copies were exported to Canada and distributed by W. J. Gage & Co.

Contains the poems "Salmon drowns eagle," "In memoriam: Ingvald Bjorndal and his comrade," "[Cain shall not slay Abel today on our good ground]," "[King Lear blinded Oedipus in a dream]," "[The world of ghosts moves closer every hour]," "Lupus in fabula," and "[He plays the piano with a razor]," 371–375.

Note: "Salmon drowns eagle" is slightly revised from its appearance in C39 and appears, again in a slightly revised version, in *Twentieth Century Canadian Poetry*, edited by Earle Birney, Toronto, Ryerson, 1953.

"In memoriam: Ingvald Bjorndal and his comrade" is slightly revised from its appearance in C37.

A revised version of "[Cain shall not slay Abel today on our good ground]" appears in *Selected Poems* (A5) under the title "A poem of God's mercy."

For a history of the title "Lupus in fabula" see C47.

"[He plays the piano with a razor]" appears in *Selected Poems* (A5) in a slightly revised version under the title "The comedian."

B6 TURVEY A MILITARY PICARESQUE 1949

TURVEY | A MILITARY PICARESQUE | by | Earle Birney | (rule) | (publisher's logo) | Toronto | McClelland & Stewart Limited

[i–x] 1–[294]. $7^{7}/_{8} \times 5^{1}/_{4}$ inches. Red cloth lettered in black on spine. White endpapers. White dust jacket printed in red, black, and brown.

Published October 1949 at $3.25. Production records not available. First printing stated on copyright page.

Contains a five-line blurb by Lowry on rear flap of dust jacket. The blurb is a quote from C53.

Note: Turvey was first published in England by Abelard-Schuman in 1958, and copies were exported to the United States with the same "London and New York" imprint. This English edition contains a longer Lowry quote than B6 on the back panel of the dust jacket. First printing stated on copyright page.

B7 A LONG DAY'S DYING 1950

FREDERICK BUECHNER | A | LONG DAY'S | DYING | (publisher's logo) | ALFRED A. KNOPF: NEW YORK | 1950

[i–x] [1]–[270]. $7^{1}/_{2} \times 5$ inches. Black cloth lettered in copper down spine; blindstamped on front and back covers. White endpapers. Top edge stained orange; fore edge untrimmed. Black and orange dust jacket printed in orange, white and black with a photograph of author on back panel.

Published 6 January 1950 at $3.00. Production records do not indicate number of printings, but 14,500 copies were sold, indicating a total printing of about 15,000 copies. First printing stated on copyright page.

Contains a ten-line blurb by Lowry on rear panel of dust jacket. See also A3.

Note: There were advance copies in wrappers, but neither these nor the English edition have the Lowry blurb.

B8 CANADIAN ANTHOLOGY 1955

CANADIAN ANTHOLOGY | C.F. KLINCK | *University of Western Ontario* | R.E. WATTERS | *University of British Columbia* | W. J. GAGE AND COMPANY LIMITED • TORONTO (with a perpendicular broken rule running through title and names of editors)

[i–xviii] 1–558. 9 1/4 × 6 7/16 inches. Green cloth lettered horizontally in gilt on front cover and spine. White endpapers. Dust jacket not seen.

Published 1950. Production records not available. First printing not stated on copyright page.

Contains the first book printing of the short story "Strange Comfort Afforded by the Profession," 410–421.

B9 BRITISH COLUMBIA: A CENTENNIAL ANTHOLOGY 1958

(Double title page) *British Columbia*: (list of members of "Editorial Advisory Board" running from top to bottom of page) *a Centennial Anthology* | *Reginald Eyre Watters,* EDITOR-IN-CHIEF | *McClelland and Stewart Limited:* 1958 | (decoration).

[i]–xvi 1–576. 9 × 5 3/4 inches. There were four bindings with no priority as follows.

1. Trade edition: blue/gray cloth lettered horizontally on spine in gilt on two black rectangular backgrounds and with decorations in gilt. Gilt decoration in a square black background on front cover. Map endpapers. Blue dust jacket lettered in black, red, and white and with an overall gilt scroll decoration. White background panels

on front and back panels and spine; the one on the front panel contains an Indian design in black, red, and blue; the one on the back panel contains a map of British Columbia decorated in black, red, and blue; the one on the spine contains a gilt scroll design. Page [i] blank. In some copies of this edition, however, page [i] states "*This copy of the first edition of* British Columbia: A Centennial Anthology *is presented with the compliments of The British Columbia Centennial Committee 1958.*" These copies also have a 'compliments' card loosely inserted.

2. Deluxe edition I. Gray cloth; quarter brown leather; lettered horizontally in gilt on spine and with gilt decoration on front and back covers. No dust jacket. Enclosed in a paper box similar to the dust jacket of the trade edition but using a buff background. Page [i] of this edition lettered "To (name written in ink) with the compliments of the Bank of Montreal." It seems quite possible that all 350 copies in this binding were not taken by the same firm. These copies sold for $12.50 each.

3. Deluxe edition II. 30 copies were bound in deluxe calfskin and sold for $35.00 each. I have not located a copy of this edition.

4. Deluxe edition III. 30 copies were bound in full morocco and sold for $17.50 each. I have not located a copy of this edition.

Published 14 May 1958. There was a total printing of 35,375 copies. There was a reprint, in paperback, of 985 copies at $5.95 on 23 June 1961, but these may have been unbound sheets of the first printing.

Contains the first book printing of the short story "The Bravest Boat," 185–197.

Note: The text of the trade edition is printed in black and blue, whereas the Deluxe edition I is printed in black and red.

B10 WINTER'S TALES 11 1965

WINTER'S TALES | 11 | Edited by | *A. D. Maclean* | MACMILLAN | London • Melbourne • Toronto | (rule) | ST MARTIN'S PRESS | New York | 1965

[i–viii] 1–[216]. 7$^{3}/_{4}$ × 4$^{15}/_{16}$ inches. Medium blue paper boards lettered in gilt horizontally on spine. White endpapers. White dust jacket printed in an overall abstract design in red and blue and lettered in white on a red background; flaps printed in red and black.

Published October 1965 at 21*s*. Print run was 3,000 copies, of which 1,000 were for the American market and had the St. Martin's Press imprint at base of spine of book and dust jacket. First printing not stated on copyright page.

Contains the short story "The Element Follows You Around, Sir!" 83–119.

B11 LONDON MAGAZINE POEMS 1961–66 1966

London Magazine Poems | 1961–66 | Selected by Hugo Williams, with an | introduction by Alan Ross | Alan Ross *London 1966*

[1]–[224]. 7$^{3}/_{16}$ × 3$^{1}/_{2}$ inches. Buff paper wrappers lettered in green.

Published November 1966 at 6*s*6*d*. Production records not available but the publisher believes that about 2,000 copies were printed. There was no second printing. Printing stated on copyright page (p. 221).

Contains the poems "Look out! The bloody bosun!" "Byzantium," and "Visiting the wreck: An able seaman explains," 68–70, the last being the first book publication, the first two having appeared in *Selected Poems*, 1962 (A5).

B12 CANADIAN WINTER'S TALES 1968

CANADIAN | *WINTER'S* | *TALES* | *Edited by Norman Levine* | *Macmillan of Canada / Toronto* | *Macmillan & Co Ltd / London*

[i–x] 1–[174]. 8 × 4 7/8 inches. Red cloth printed in white. White endpapers. Red and purple dust jacket printed in white and black.

5,000 copies published in September 1968 at $4.25. Of this number, 1,500 copies were exported to the U.K. The only difference between the Canadian and the U.K. editions was the Macmillan logo on the dust jacket. There was a second printing, in paperback, of 2,000 copies in 1972.

Contains the first book printing of the short story version of "Under the Volcano," 1–21.

Note: The short story "Under the Volcano" was later developed into chapter VIII of the novel *Under the Volcano*.

B13 THE PRIVATÉ LABYRINTH OF MALCOLM LOWRY 1969

THE | PRIVATE | LABYRINTH | OF | MALCOLM | LOWRY | *UNDER THE VOLCANO* | AND THE CABBALA | BY | PERLE S. EPSTEIN | Holt, Rinehart and Winston | *New York Chicago San Francisco*

[i]–[x] [1]–[246]. 8 1/8 × 5 1/4 inches. Black cloth, spine lettered in gilt. White endpapers. Black dust jacket lettered in white, red, and brown with portrait of author on rear panel.

Published July 1969 at $6.95. Production details not available. First printing stated on copyright page.

Contains excerpts from Lowry's previously unpublished journal notes on two of his stories; the "Outward Bound" chapter from *October Ferry to Gabriola* and "Ghostkeeper," 225–228.

Note: Advance copies in wrappers were issued.

B14 MALCOLM LOWRY: THE MAN AND HIS WORK 1971

MALCOLM LOWRY: | THE MAN AND HIS WORK | *edited by* | GEORGE WOODCOCK | University of British Columbia Press | *Vancouver*

[i–x] 1–174. 9¾ × 6¾ inches. Coated white paper wrappers printed in light and dark green and black.

Published July 1971 at $4.50. Reprinted May 1972 and October 1973. Each printing, 1,000 copies. Printings stated on copyright page.

Contains "Preface to a Novel," 9–15, reprinted from *Canadian Literature* #9 (C125).

Contains the following poems, all reprinted from *Canadian Literature* #8 (C81–89), "A lament—June 1944," "In tempest's tavern," "After publication of *Under the Volcano*," "Hypocrisy," "Lupus in fabula," "The dodder," "Autopsy," "Strange type," and "Joseph Conrad," 94–98. All but the third and the eighth are first book printings.

Contains "Two Letters," to Albert Erskine and David Markson, 110–116, reprinted from *Canadian Literature* #44 (C216–217)

Note: See C125 for publishing history of "Preface to a Novel" and C47 for a history of the title "Lupus in fabula."

B15 MALCOLM LOWRY A BIOGRAPHY 1973

Malcolm | *Lowry* [in script] | A BIOGRAPHY BY DOUGLAS DAY | New York OXFORD UNIVERSITY PRESS 1973

[i–xvi] [1]–[488]. 8⅞ × 5¾ inches. Black cloth with a violet strip at bottom, lettered in two shades of gold on spine and blind-stamped on front cover. Orange-red endpapers. White dust jacket lettered in red, black, and purple and with a reproduction of a painting by Albert Pinkham Ryder in shades of green, yellow, and black on front panel; black and white photograph of Lowry on rear panel.

Published November 1973 at $10.00. Production records not available. First printing not stated on copyright page.

Contains the following quotes, excerpts, etc., some of which are previously unpublished, the others not having previously appeared in a book.

Quotes from letters to David Markson (Nov 1954), 12; (May 1954), 192–193; (20 May 1954), 463.
letter to Giorgio and Daniela Monicelli (Nov 1954), 12.
letter to Doris Lewis (Sept 1929), 108–109.
letter to Clemens ten Holder (31 Oct 1951), 116.
letter to John Davenport (1936), 234–236. (An abridged version of this letter appears in *Selected Letters,* 11–13.)
letters to his father (1938), 237–238; (22 Apr 1940), 275; (26 May 1942), 297.
letter to an unidentified "Alfred" in Mexico City, 238n.
letter to Antonio, manager of the Hotel Francia in Oaxaca (1937), 243
letters to James Stern (Feb 1947), 379; (23 Mar 1947), 384.

Quotes from the manuscripts of *The Ordeal of Sigbjorn Wilderness,* 78, 140.
Dark as the Grave, 142–143.
Under the Volcano (second draft), 259, 262–269.
Under the Volcano (third draft), 273.
La Mordida, 356, 360, 363, 370.

Quotes from Lowry's Haitian notebooks, 371, 377, and reproduces four pages, 378.

Quotes from Lowry's journal for 7 Nov 1947, 392.

Quotes from Lowry's written resolution to cut down on his drinking, "Resolution of the Higher Self" (Jan/Feb 1949), 413.

Quotes from Lowry's "work in progress' statement sent to Harold Matson (22 Nov 1951), 426–427, 444.

Quotes from the essay "Garden of Etla," 240–243 and the poem "Reflection to windward," 283.

Reprints from C169 the poem "Self-pity," 283–284.

Reproduces a pencil sketch by Lowry, 92.

Quotes excerpts from the following issues of *The Leys Fortnightly:*
(12 Feb 1926) short story "Satan in a Barrel," 82; reports on school hockey games, 83.
(26 Feb 1926) letter to the editor, 83–84.

(29 Oct 1926) review of school performance of *Macbeth*, 85.
(26 Nov 1926) poem "The rain fell heavily," 84.
(16 Dec 1926) letter to the editor, 85.

Note: Advance copies in wrappers were issued.

Note: The English edition was published by Oxford University Press in April 1974. Bound copies were imported from the United States. These copies are identical to the American edition with the exception of the title page, copyright page, and dust jacket. The English dust jacket is lettered in white and green on a black background on the front panel and spine and reproduces the same Albert Pinkham Ryder painting. The back panel reproduces a black and white photograph (different from the one used on the American jacket) of Lowry and is lettered in white on a black background with a 13-line quotation from an unpublished journal of Lowry beginning "Death of a sense of fun." Flaps lettered in black on a white background.

B16 LOWRY 1973

LOWRY | (decorative rule) | TONY KILGALLIN | (drawing of scorpion) | 1973

[1]–[232]. Frontispiece and tissue guard tipped in facing title page. Errata & addenda sheet. 7 1/4 × 5 5/8 inches. Red padded "Tanotex" cover lettered in white on spine and with a scorpion in white on top cover. Issued without dust jacket. Black and blue-gray endpapers illustrated with an astrologic theme.

Published September 1973 at $8.95 by Press Porcepic, Erin, Ontario. Publisher's records no longer available but printer states press run probably between 500 and 1,000. "Published . . . September of 1973" on copyright page.

Contains untitled song lyric by Lowry, "Rich man, poor man, beggarman, thief," 23 (a more complete version than that in Charlotte Haldane's *I Bring Not Peace,* B3); the "twelve-point program" that Lowry gave to Charles Stansfeld-Jones, 47–51; an excerpt from the then unpublished story "China," 87; a brief note that Lowry attached to the galleys of *Under the Volcano*, 149–150.

B17 MALCOLM LOWRY 1974
HIS ART & EARLY LIFE

MALCOLM LOWRY | HIS ART & EARLY LIFE | A study in transformation | M.C. BRADBROOK | Mistress of Girton College and Professor of | English in the University of Cambridge | CAMBRIDGE UNIVERSITY PRESS

[i–xiv] 1–170. 7 3/4 × 4 15/16 inches. Black paper boards lettered in gilt down spine. White endpapers. White dust jacket printed in black and brown.

Published 18 July 1974 at £2.50 in U.K. and $6.95 in the U.S.; 2,500 copies printed. A paper edition was published 31 July 1975, 2,000 copies printed. First printing stated on copyright page.

Contains two short stories: "A Rainy Night," 138, and "Satan in a Barrel," 144, both reprinted from *The Leys Fortnightly.*

B18 MALCOLM LOWRY: 1975
PSALMS AND SONGS

Malcolm Lowry: | Psalms and Songs | EDITED BY | *Margerie Lowry* | (publisher's logo) | A MERIDIAN BOOK | NEW AMERICAN LIBRARY | (rule) | TIMES MIRROR | NEW YORK AND SCARBOROUGH, ONTARIO

[i]–xii [1]–308. 7 7/8 × 5 1/4 inches. Paper wrappers printed in light brown, orange, and blue on a brown photographic background on front cover and spine; lettered in orange, blue, and dark brown on a white ground on back cover.

Published October 1975 at $5.95. First printing stated on copyright page and numeral 1 used in ascending-numeral method. Production information not available, but went into a second printing, which is indicated by the numeral 2. First printing notice not removed on this second printing. Remaindered late 1982.

Contains the short stories "Seductio ad Absurdum," 3–18; "Hotel Room in Chartres," 19–24; "On Board the West Hardaway," 25–35; "June the 30th, 1934," 36–48; "China," 49–54; "Under the Volcano," 187–201; "Ghostkeeper," 202–227; "Enter One in Sumptuous Armour," 228–249; "Kristbjorg's Story: In the Black Hills," 250–253; "Lunar Caustic," 259–306. The second, third, fourth, seventh, and eighth are first book printings.

Contains: Downie Kirk's article "More Than Music: Glimpses of Malcolm Lowry," 112–119, reprinted from *Canadian Literature* #8 (C90), which quotes from several Lowry letters.

Contains: James Stern's article "Malcolm Lowry: A First Impression," 72–86, reprinted from *Encounter*, September 1967 (C213), which prints a postcard sent by Lowry to Stern in early 1947.

Contains: A. C. Nyland's "Malcolm Lowry: The Writer," 139–184 (chapter 2 of an unpublished doctoral thesis, *The Luminous Wheel: the Evolution of Malcolm Lowry's Style*), which quotes from the early stories "Travelling Light," "The Repulsive Tragedy of the Incredulous Englishman," "The Blue Bonnet," "A Rainy Night," and "Satan in a Barrel"; from the poems "The old woman who buried cats," "The rain fell heavily," "Number 8 fireman," "In memoriam: Ingvald Bjorndal," "Indian Arm," "The unborn," and "One flying line"; from Lowry's reports on hockey games and from one of his letters to the editor of *The Leys Fortnightly*; and from Lowry's letters to Conrad Aiken.

Note: "On Board the West Hardaway" is a reworked and lengthened version of "Port Swettenham." It was again reworked to become Chapter V of *Ultramarine.*

Note: "Seductio ad Absurdum" is a slightly revised version of "Punctum Indifferens Skibet Gaar Videre." It was later rewritten and used as chapter IV of *Ultramarine.*

Note: The short story "Under the Volcano" was later developed into chapter VIII of the novel of the same name.

B19 MALCOLM LOWRY AND THE VOYAGE THAT NEVER ENDS 1976

David Miller | *Malcolm Lowry and the Voyage that Never Ends* | London / Enitharmon Press / 1976

[1]–[64]. 8 3/16 × 5 11/16 inches. Issued in three states as below.

1. Fifty numbered copies on Glastonbury Antique Sage Green paper signed by author. Beige linen cloth lettered in brown down spine. Green endpapers. Top edge gilt. Unprinted glassine dust jacket. This issue is larger than the trade issue, measuring 8 7/16 × 5 3/4 inches.
2. Trade issue, cloth. Brown cloth lettered in gilt down spine. White endpapers. Green dust jacket printed in black.
3. Trade issue, paper. Blue paper wrappers, unprinted. Dust jacket as on trade issue, cloth. This issue contains two extra blank leaves at front and two at rear.

All issues contain a frontispiece inserted before title page and a photograph of Lowry inserted after contents page.

Published 28 January 1977. Fifty numbered copies on green paper at £12.00; trade issue, cloth, 300 copies at £2.70; and trade issue, paper, 450 copies at £1.80. First printing stated on copyright page.

Contains as a frontispiece a photographic reproduction of the first page of the typescript of the unfinished novel *La Mordida*.

B20 THE ART OF MALCOLM LOWRY 1978

THE ART OF | MALCOLM LOWRY | edited by | Anne Smith | Vision

[1]–[176]. 8 7/16 × 5 1/4 inches. Pink paper boards lettered in gilt on spine. White endpapers. White dust jacket lettered in white and black on a pink background on front panel and spine and with a black and white photograph of Lowry on front panel; lettered in black on rear panel and flaps on a white ground.

Published by Vision Press, London, 31 August 1978 at £5.40; 2,250 copies printed.

Contains quotations from the early manuscripts of *Under the Volcano* in Brian O'Kill's essay "Aspects of Language in *Under the Volcano*," 72. M. C. Bradbrook's essay "Intention and Design in 'October Ferry to Gabriola'," 144, quotes from Lowry's "work in progress," a 60-odd page typescript sent to his agent in 1951 and now at the University of British Columbia Library.

B21 MALCOLM LOWRY 1980
A PREFACE TO HIS FICTION

Malcolm Lowry | A Preface to His Fiction | Richard | K. | Cross | The | University of Chicago Press | Chicago and London

[i]–[xiv] 1–146. $7^{7}/_{16} \times 5^{1}/_{4}$ inches. Medium orange paper boards lettered in silver on spine. Beige endpapers. White dust jacket printed in white and pink on a brown background on both panels and spine and with a skeleton-like figure in dark pink on front panel; front flap lettered in brown and pink on a white ground and back flap lettered in brown on a white ground.

1,500 copies published February 1980 at $12.50.

Contains material from unpublished manuscripts in the collection at the University of British Columbia Library:
—quotes from the manuscript of *La Mordida*, 135; from the manuscript of *Dark as the Grave Wherein My Friend Is Laid*, 132, and from the notes for this manuscript, 133–134; from the 1940 draft of *Under the Volcano*, 48, 129; from the notes for *In Ballast to the White Sea*, 8, 15; from a memorandum to Margerie Lowry about *October Ferry to Gabriola,* 136.
—quotes from unpublished letters to Conrad Aiken (early 1930s), 115; to Albert Erskine (14 October 1953), 140, and (December 1953), 76, 81, 83, 137; to Robert Giroux (11 January 1952), 114; to Harold Matson (4 October 1940), 65, and (November 1951), 139; to Arabel Porter (29 May 1953), 130; and from an unfinished letter to Giorgio Monicelli (1955), 137.

B22 THE VOYAGE THAT NEVER ENDS 1982

THE VOYAGE | THAT NEVER ENDS | MALCOLM LOWRY'S FICTION | SHERRILL E. GRACE | UNIVERSITY OF BRITISH COLUMBIA PRESS | VANCOUVER

[i]–xvi 1–152. 9 × 5¾ inches. Black paper boards lettered down spine in gilt. White endpapers. White dust jacket printed in brown and black.

Published 29 November 1982. 1,200 hardcover copies published at $24.00 (Canadian) and 800 paperback copies published at $9.95 (Canadian). First printing not stated on copyright page.

Contains material from unpublished manuscripts in the collection at the University of British Columbia Library:
—quotes from Lowry's "Work in Progress" statement throughout the first chapter.
—reproduces a page of typescript from *The Ordeal of Sigbjorn Wilderness*, 10.
—quotes from the original manuscript of the "Perilous Chapel" chapter of *October Ferry to Gabriola*, 18; reproduces a page of typescript, 17 and on the dust jacket.
—quotes from Lowry's notes for *Lunar Caustic*, 13–14, 30; notes for first complete novel version, 1940, of *Under the Volcano*, 39–40, 43–44; notes for *La Mordida*, 60–61; notes for *Dark as the Grave Wherein My Friend Is Laid*, 62, 65; notes for *October Ferry to Gabriola*, 88–91, 96, 98, 137–138; quotes a nine-line poem beginning "Schoolbells toll from the invisible coast wise railway across the bay," from notes for *Present Estate of Pompeii*, 99; notes for *Through the Panama*, 104; notes for *Elephant and Colosseum*, 110.
—quotes from an unpublished letter to Albert Erskine (December 1953), 76, 77, 90, 95, 97–98.

SECTION C
Contributions to Periodicals

C. Contributions to Periodicals

Index to Periodicals in Section C

C14, October 15 C15, October 29 C16, November 26 C17, December 16 C18
1927 February 18 C19, December 15 C22
1928 May 18 C23, June 1 C24
Life and Letters
1934 July C32
London Daily Mail
1927 September 30 C21
London Evening News
1927 May 14 C20
London Magazine
1961 December C154–156
MacLean's Magazine
1961 July 15 C113
A Malcolm Lowry Catalogue
1968 C214–215
Massachusetts Review
1961 Spring C93–95
The Minnesota Review
1961 Fall C148
Moment
1960 March C63, April C64
Nation
1966 February 7 C212
New World Writing
1953 C58
1961 March C75
The New Yorker
1962 May 5 C185
The New York Times
1959 October 11 C61, December 1 C62
1961 September 17 C124
Northwest Review
1962 Winter C173–184
Outposts
1948 Summer C48
Paris Review
1960 Spring C65
1961 Summer/Fall C129–131
1963 Winter/Spring C199
Partisan Review
1954 May/June C59
1959 Spring C60
Perspective
1962 Spring C192–193
Prairie Schooner
1963/64 Winter C200–206
Prism International
1965 Summer C209
Queen's Quarterly
1961 Autumn C149–151
Raven
1962 March C166–167
Review of English Literature
1961 October C132
Saturday Review
1962 January 6 C158
Shenandoah
1964 Spring C208
Show Magazine
1964 March C207
Sotheby & Co.
1976 December 17 C221
Southwest Review
1962 Summer C198
Story
1933 October C31
1934 September C33
Tamarack Review
1961 Spring C96–112
1962 Spring C194–196
Thunderbird
1949December C53
United Nations World
1950 June C56
Vancouver Daily Province
1939 December 12 C34, December 13 C35, December 29 C36

Vancouver Sun
1961 March 16 C76
Varsity
1931 May 9 C29
The Venture
1930 June C27
Virginia Quarterly Review
1961 Summer C126—128
Wake
1952 C57
Western Humanities Review
1961 Autumn C152–153
White Pelican
1974 Spring C220
X:A Quarterly Review
1961 August C120–123

1925

C1 THE LIGHT THAT FAILED NOT. *The Leys Fortnightly,* The Leys School, Cambridge, XLIX, 861 (13 March 1925) 165–167.
Short story signed 'Camel.'

C2 DER TAG. *The Leys Fortnightly*, XLIX, 862 (1 April 1925), 186.
Poem signed 'Camel.'

C3 TRAVELLING LIGHT. *The Leys Fortnightly,* XLIX, 865 (18 June 1925), 255–257.
Short story signed 'Camel.'

C4 THE BLUE BONNET. *The Leys Fortnightly,* L, 869 (9 October 1925), 5–7.
Short story signed 'Camel.'

C5 A RAINY NIGHT. *The Leys Fortnightly,* L, 870 (23 October 1925), 35–40.
Short story signed 'Camel.'

1926

C6 SATAN IN A BARREL. *The Leys Fortnightly,* L, 876 (12 February 1926), 134–138.
Short story signed 'Camel.'

C7 Reports on school hockey games. *The Leys Fortnightly,* L, 876 (12 February 1926), 141–143
Leys v. Royal Dental Hospital, January 30.
Leys v. Cambridge M.A.'s, February 2.
Leys v. The Sloths, February 4.

Leys v. Peterhouse, February 6.
All signed 'C.M.L.'

C8 HOMOEOPATHIC BLUES IN J. *The Leys Fortnightly*, L, 877 (26 February 1926), 150.
Poem signed 'Camel.'

C9 Letter to the editor. *The Leys Fortnightly*, L, 877 (26 February 1926), 157–158.
Replying to letters criticizing his stories. Signed 'Camel.'

C10 Reports on school hockey games. *The Leys Fortnightly,* L, 877 (26 February 1926), 158–160.
Leys v. Christ's, February 13.
Leys v. St. John's, February 16.
Leys v. Felsted, February 20.
All signed 'C.M.L.'

C11 Reports on school hockey games. *The Leys Fortnightly*, L, 878 (12 March 1926), 178–181.
Leys v. Old Leysians, February 27.
Leys v. Mill Hill, March 6 (unsigned but apparently by C.M.L.).
Leys v. Cambridge University Wanderers, March 4.
All signed 'C.M.L.' except as noted.

C12 Reports on school hockey games. *The Leys Fortnightly*, L, 879 (29 March 1926), 205–207.
Leys v. Cranleigh, March 13.
Leys v. Guy's, March 11.
Both signed 'C.M.L.'
This issue also contains a review of the play *Tilly of Bloomsbury* in which Lowry appeared as Percy, 193.

C13 Reports on school hockey games. *The Leys Fortnightly,* L, 880 (7 May 1926), 228–231.
Leys v. Sporting Club de Colombes, April 2.
Leys v. Standard A.C., April 5.
Leys v. Paris University, undated.
All signed 'C.M.L.'

C14 THE REPULSIVE TRAGEDY OF THE INCREDULOUS ENGLISHMAN. *The Leys Fortnightly*, L, 882 (4 June 1926), 255–259.
Short story signed 'Camel.'

C15 THE OLD WOMAN WHO BURIED CATS. *The Leys Fortnightly*, LI, 888 (15 October 1926), 26–27.
Poem signed 'Camel.'

C16 "MACBETH." BY WM. SHAKESPEARE. *The Leys Fortnightly*, LI, 889 (29 October 1926), 43–44.
Review of a school performance. Signed 'Camel.'
This issue also contains a report on the "Literary and Debating Society" on page 45. "The best paper was that of C. M. Lowry . . ."

C17 THE RAIN FELL HEAVILY. *The Leys Fortnightly*, LI, 891 (26 November 1926), 78–79.
Poem signed 'Camel.;

C18 Letter to the editor. *The Leys Fortnightly*, LI, 892 (16 December 1926), 109–110.
Replying to an article on an Old Leysian Debate "Public School men are better than self-made men." Signed 'Camel.'

1927

C19 Report on school hockey game. *The Leys Fortnightly*, LI, 894 (18 February 1927), 160–161.
First XI v. Essex Regiment, February 15.
Signed 'C.M.L.'

C20 "Rich Boy as Deck Hand." *London Evening News*, 14 May 1927, 5.
Interview with Lowry and his mother by the paper's Liverpool correspondent at the time of Lowry's sailing on the S.S. *Pyrrhus*.

C21 "Once Quite Enough. Cotton Broker's Son as Deckhand." *London Daily Mail*, 30 September 1927, 9.
Interview with Lowry after his return on the S.S. *Pyrrhus*.

C22 THE GLORY OF THE SEA. *The Leys Fortnightly*, LII, 909 (15 December 1927), 94–95.
Poem signed 'Camel.'

1928

C23 THE COOK IN THE GALLEY. *The Leys Fortnightly*, LII, 915 (18 May 1928), 230.
Poem signed 'Camel.'

C24 NUMBER 8 FIREMAN. *The Leys Fortnightly*, LII, 916 (1 June 1928), 256–257.
Poem signed 'Camel.'

1930

C25 PORT SWETTENHAM. *Experiment*, Trinity College, Cambridge, no. 5 (February 1930), 22–26.
Short story. See note to C31.

C26 IN CAPE COD WITH CONRAD AITKEN (*sic*). *The Festival Theatre Programme*, Cambridge, I, 16 (8 March 1930), 10.
Poem.

C27 GOYA THE OBSCURE. *The Venture*, Cambridge, no. 6 (June 1930), 270–278.
Short story.

1931

C28 THOSE COKES TO NEWCASTLE BLUES. *The Festival Theatre Review*, Cambridge, IV, 68 (14 February 1931), 8–9.
Poem, signed "Conrad Aiken. Malcolm Lowry."

C29 Letter to the editor. *Varsity*, Cambridge, 9 May 1931, 2. Protests against the paper's exposure of 'the petty offences of undergraduates,' e.g., drunken driving. Signatories were Lowry, John Davenport, P. J. Macdonald, Paul Marx, Arthur Tillotson, John Palmer, and John Green.

C30 PUNCTUM INDIFFERENS SKIBET GAAR VIDERE. *Experiment* no 7 (Spring 1931), 62–75.
Short story. See note to B2.

1933

C31 ON BOARD THE WEST HARDAWAY. *Story*, New York, III, 15 (October 1933), 12–22.
Short story. A reworked and lengthened version of C25. It was again reworked to become Chapter V of *Ultramarine*, which was published in June 1933.

1934

C32 IN LE HAVRE. *Life and Letters,* London, X, 55 (July 1934), 462–466.
Short story.

C33 HOTEL ROOM IN CHARTRES. *Story*, V, 26 (September 1934), 53–58.
Short story.

1939

C34 HOLLYWOOD AND THE WAR. *Vancouver Daily Province,* no. 221, 12 December 1939, 4.
Article. Signed 'C.M.L.'

C35 THE REAL MR. CHIPS. *Vancouver Daily Province*, no. 222, 13 December 1939, 4.
Article.

C36 WHERE DID THAT ONE GO TO, 'ERBERT? *Vancouver Daily Province,* no. 235, 29 December 1939, 4.
Poem.

1941

C37 IN MEMORIAM: INGVALD BJORNDAL. *The Atlantic Monthly,* Boston, CLXVIII, 4 (October 1941), 501.
Poem. Signed 'Malcolm Boden Lowry.' A melody which Lowry composed for this poem and sang to guitar accompaniment was apparently not recorded. Reprinted in A. J. M. Smith's *A Book of Canadian Poetry,* 2nd ed. rev., 1948 (B5) with altered title and some revisions.

1947

C38 SESTINA IN A CANTINA. *Canadian Poetry Magazine*, Toronto, XI, 1 (September 1947), 24–27.
Poem. Reprinted in C49 and *Selected Poems* with stanzas rearranged and with some revisions.

C39 SALMON DROWNS EAGLE. *Contemporary Verse*, Caulfield, B.C., no. 21 (Summer 1947), 3.
Poem. Based on a story told to Lowry by 'Old Sam,' a Dollarton

squatter. Lowry retells the fable in "The Forest Path to the Spring." Reprinted, slightly revised, in A. J. M. Smith's *A Book of Canadian Poetry*, 2nd ed. rev., 1948 (B5).

C40 THE GLAUCOUS WINGED GULL. *Contemporary Verse*, no. 21 (Summer 1947), 4.
Poem. The version in A5 and D31 alters the first line and adds a new second line.

C41 STOKER TOM'S UKELELE. *Contemporary Verse*, no. 21 (Summer 1947), 4. Poem.

C42 [The poignance of a quarrel in the post!] *Contemporary Verse*, no. 21 (Summer 1947), 5.
Untitled poem. This and C43 are published under the overall title "Two poems." Reprinted, with some revisions, in *Selected Poems* (A5) under the title "A Quarrel."

C43 [This evening Venus sings alone.] *Contemporary Verse*, no. 21 (Summer 1947), 5.
Untitled poem. See note to C42. Reprinted in C50 and *Selected Poems* (A5) under the title "Nocturne."

C44 OLD FREIGHTER IN AN OLD PORT. *Canadian Poetry Magazine*, XI, 2 (December 1947), 24.
Poem.

C45 PORT MOODY. *Canadian Poetry Magazine*, XI, 2 (December 1947), 25.
Poem

C46 INDIAN ARM. *Canadian Poetry Magazine*, XI, 2 (December 1947), 25.
Poem.

1948

C47 [These animals that follow us in dream.] *Contemporary Verse*, no. 24 (Spring 1948), 6.
Untitled poem. Reprinted, with minor revisions, in A. J. M. Smith's *A Book of Canadian Poetry*, 2nd rev. ed., 1948 (B5) under the title "Lupus in Fabula." A later version then appeared in *Selected Poems* under the title "Xochitepec." In the meantime, the

title "Lupus in Fabula" had been assigned to the poem beginning "Wolf, wolf, cried the boy in the fable," which appeared in *Canadian Literature* no. 8 (C85) (Spring 1961) and in George Woodcock's *Malcolm Lowry: The Man and His Work*, 1971 (B14).

C48 SUNRISE. *Outposts*, London, no. 10 (Summer 1948), 7.
Poem.

1949

C49 SESTINA IN A CANTINA. *Arena*, London, no. 1 (Summer 1949), 79–80.
Poem. A reprint of C38, lacking the scene description, but with the stanzas in the rearranged order.

C50 NOCTURNE. *Arena*, no. 1 (Summer 1949), 81.
Poem. See note to C43.

C51 GLAUCOUS WINGED GULL. *Arena*, no. 1 (Summer 1949), 81.
Poem. A reprint of C40 with several typographical errors. The version in A5 and D31 alters the first line and adds a new second line.

C52 PORT MOODY. *Arena*, no. 1 (Summer 1949), 81.
Poem. A reprint of C45 with several typographical errors.

C53 "TURVEY" BY EARLE BIRNEY. *Thunderbird*, Vancouver, V, 1 (December 1949), 24–26.
Review of Birney's novel. Lowry's only published book review.

C54 ECONOMIC CONFERENCE 1934. *Arena*, no. 2 (Autumn 1949), 49–57.
Short story.

C55 TURNED BACK AT THE BORDER. *Arena*, no. 2 (Autumn 1949), 58–60.
Poem.

1950

C56 GARDEN OF ETLA. *United Nations World*, New York, IV, 6 (June 1950), 45–47.
Essay. Drawings by Miguel Covarrubias.

1952

C57 A LETTER. *Wake*, New York, no. 11 (no month, 1952), 80–89.
Letter to Seymour Lawrence, editor of *Wake*, for the Conrad Aiken special issue.

1953

C58 STRANGE COMFORT AFFORDED BY THE PROFESSION. *New World Writing*, New York, no. 3 (1953), 331–344.
Short story.

1954

C59 THE BRAVEST BOAT. *Partisan Review*, New York, XXI, 3 (May/June 1954), 275–288.
Short story.

1959

C60 PRESENT ESTATE OF POMPEII. *Partisan Review*, XXVI, 2 (Spring 1959), 175–199.
Short story.

C61 THE FLOWERING PAST. *The New York Times*, CIX, 37,150 (11 October 1959), section 4, p. 10E.
Poem.

C62 NO STILL PATH. *The New York Times*, CIX, 37,201 (1 December 1959), 38.
Poem.

1960

C63 TO THREE IN LONDON. *Moment*, Montreal, no. 1 (n.d., ca. March 1960), 9.
Poem. Lowry's final title was "Warning From False Cape Horn."

C64 SESTINA IN A CANTINA. *Moment*, no. 2 (April 1960), 7.
Poem. Reprinted from C38. See note to that entry.

C65 THROUGH THE PANAMA. *Paris Review*, no. 23 (Spring 1960), 87–163.

Novella. Introduced by Harvey Breit and illustrated by J. F. Ulysse.

1961

C66 [Imprisoned in a Liverpool of self.] *Contact*, Sausalito, no. 7 (February 1961), 83.
Untitled poem. Reprinted in *Selected Poems* under the title "Trinity."

C67 THE GLAUCOUS-WINGED GULL. *Contact*, no. 7 (February 1961), 84.
Poem. Reprinted from C40 and C51. The version in A5 and D31 alters the first line and adds a new second line.

C68 IN THE OAXACA GAOL. *Contact*, no. 7 (February 1961), 84.
Poem. Spelling of "gaol" is Americanized in *Selected Poems* and the poem is revised.

C69 MR. LOWRY'S DERIVATIVE GOOD FRIDAY UNDER A REAL CACTUS. *Contact*, no. 7 (February 1961), 85.
Poem.

C70 DON'T, HAVE ONE FOR THE ROAD. *Contact*, no. 7 (February 1961), 85.
Poem.

C71 EYE-OPENER. *Contact*, no. 7 (February 1961), 85.
Poem.

C72 [THE FLOWERING PAST]. *Contact*, no. 7 (February 1961), 86.
Poem. Reprinted from C61.

C73 OLD FREIGHTER IN AN OLD PORT. *Contact*, no. 7 (February 1961), 86.
Poem. Reprinted, with slight revisions, from C44.

C74 [THE PILGRIM.] *Contact*, no. 7 (February 1961) 87.
Poem.

C75 THE FOREST PATH TO THE SPRING. *New World Writing*, New York, no. 18 (March 1961), 153–221.
Short story. Issued both in paperback and in cloth with dust jacket.

C76 THE FOREST PATH TO THE SPRING. *Vancouver Sun*, LXXV, 138 (16 March 1961), 31.
Short story. Untitled extract consisting of last 800 words beginning "The wash from the invisible freighter . . ." was printed in Jack Scott's column in this issue.

C77 THE UNKNOWN POETRY OF MALCOLM LOWRY by Earle Birney. *British Columbia Library Quarterly*, Vancouver, XXIV, 4 (April 1961), 33–40.
Contains quotations from the following poems: "Reflection to windward," "Look out! The bloody bosun," "The ship is turning homeward," "Note for a poem," "The drunkards," "Prayer for drunks," "Comfort," "Reading Don Quixote," "Venus," "A new ship," "Love which comes too late," "The world of ghosts moves closer every hour," "No still path," "Be patient for the wolf," "Because of no moment," "Wind blowing through the shack," "Port Moody," "Kingfishers in British Columbia," and "To three in London."

C78 HEAT WAVE. *Hip Pocket Poems*, Hanover, N.H., no. 4 (June 1961). Unpaginated.
Poem. This issue also contains a poem by Jack Hirschman entitled "To Lowry."

C79 HARPIES. *Hip Pocket Poems*, no. 4 (June 1961). Unpaginated.
Poem. Previously published in French in *Les lettres nouvelles*, July/August 1960 (D22).

C80 WHAT SIGBJØRN SAID. Hip Pocket Poems, no. 4 (June 1961). Unpaginated.
Poem.

C81 A LAMENT—JUNE 1944. *Canadian Literature,* Vancouver, no. 8 (Spring 1961), 20.
Poem.

C82 IN TEMPEST'S TAVERN. *Canadian Literature*, no. 8 (Spring 1961), 20.
Poem.

C83 AFTER PUBLICATION OF "UNDER THE VOLCANO." *Canadian Literature*, no. 8 (Spring 1961), 21.
Poem.

C84 HYPOCRISY. *Canadian Literature*, no. 8 (Spring 1961), 21.
Poem.

C85 LUPUS IN FABULA. *Canadian Literature*, no. 8 (Spring 1961), 22.
Poem. See note to C47.

C86 THE DODDER. *Canadian Literature*, no. 8 (Spring 1961), 22.
Poem.

C87 AUTOPSY. *Canadian Literature,* no. 8 (Spring 1961), 23.
Poem.

C88 STRANGE TYPE. *Canadian Literature*, no. 8 (Spring 1961), 23.
Poem.

C89 JOSEPH CONRAD. *Canadian Literature*, no. 8 (Spring 1961), 24.
Poem.

C90 MORE THAN MUSIC GLIMPSES OF MALCOLM LOWRY by Downie Kirk. *Canadian Literature,* no. 8 (Spring 1961), 31–38.
Kirk's article quotes from Lowry letters. Kirk was Lowry's neighbor at Dollarton.

C91 Letter to Albert Erskine. *Canadian Literature*, no. 8 (Spring 1961), 39–42. Undated letter, beginning "Dear Albert, Your letter arrived without hitch . . ." Previously printed in French in *Les lettres nouvelles,* July/August 1960 (D22). Not in *Selected Letters.*

C92 Letter to David Markson. *Canadian Literature*, no. 8 (Spring 1961), 42–46. Undated, but postmarked 20 May 1954, letter, beginning "Dear old Dave, Hold that note, Roland . . ." An extract of this letter was previously printed in French in *Les lettres nouvelles,* July/August 1960 (D22). Not in *Selected Letters.*

C93 THE DEVIL'S KITCHEN. *Massachusetts Review*, Amherst, II, 3 (Spring 1961), 412.
Poem.

C94 THE EXILE. *Massachusetts Review*, II, 3 (Spring 1961), 412–413.
Poem.

C95 BOSUN'S SONG. *Massachusetts Review*, II, 3 (Spring 1961), 413.
Poem.

C96 [BECAUSE OF NO MOMENT.] *Tamarack Review*, Toronto, no. 19 (Spring 1961), 42.
Poem.

C97 [THE VOLCANO IS DARK.] *Tamarack Review*, no. 19 (Spring 1961), 43.
Poem.

C98 [THE PATHS OF WOLVES.] *Tamarack Review*, no. 19 (Spring 1961), 43.
Poem.

C99 VIGIL FORGET. *Tamarack Review,* no. 19 (Spring 1961), 44.
Poem.

C100 CHRIST WALKS IN THIS INFERNAL DISTRICT TOO. *Tamarack Review,* no. 19 (Spring 1961), 44.
Poem.

C101 ALTERNATIVE. *Tamarack Review*, no. 19 (Spring 1961), 45.
Poem.

C102 DRAFT BOARD. Tamarack Review, no. 19 (Spring 1961), 45.
Poem.

C103 THE DOLLARTON BUS STOP. *Tamarack Review*, no. 19 (Spring 1961), 45.
Poem.

C104 [BLANK SONNET.] *Tamarack Review*, no. 19 (Spring 1961), 46.
Untitled poem beginning "There is a tide in the affairs of men."

C105 BLEPHARIPÁPPUS GLANDULOSUS OR WHITE TIDY-TIPS. *Tamarack Review*, no. 19 (Spring 1961), 46.
Poem.

C106 [FRAGMENT.] *Tamarack Review*, no. 19 (Spring 1961), 47.
Untitled poem beginning "A wounded voice over the telephone . . ."

C107 JOKES IN THE GALLEY. *Tamarack Review,* no. 19 (Spring 1961), 48.
Poem.

C108 LINES ON THE POET BEING INFORMED THAT HIS EPIC ABOUT THE PHILISTINES &c NEEDED CUTTING. *Tamarack Review*, no. 19 (Spring 1961), 48.
Poem.

C109 NOTE FOR A POEM. *Tamarack Review*, no. 19 (Spring 1961), 48.
Poem.

C110 [The dead man sat in the sun.] *Tamarack Review*, no. 19 (Spring 1961), 49.
Untitled poem.

C111 NO TIME TO STOP AND THINK. *Tamarack Review*, no. 19 (Spring 1961), 49.
Poem. Previously published in French in *Les lettres nouvelles*, July/August 1960 (D22).

C112 [SEMICOLON TECHNIQUE.] *Tamarack Review*, no. 19 (Spring 1961), 49.
Poem.

C113 THE FOREST PATH TO THE SPRING. *MacLean's Magazine*, Toronto, LXXIV, 14 (15 July 1961), 18.
An abbreviated version of this short story.

C114 THE MAGIC WORLD. *Canadian Forum*, Toronto, XLI, 487 (August 1961), 112.
Poem.

C115 SONG. *Canadian Forum*, XLI, 487 (August 1961), 112.
Poem.

C116 TASHTEGO BELIEVED RED. *Canadian Forum*, XLI, 487 (August 1961), 112.
Poem.

C117 NOCTURNE IN BURRARD INLET. *Canadian Forum*, XLI, 487 (August 1961), 112.
Poem.

C118 DOGGEREL. *Canadian Forum*, XLI 487 (August 1961), 112–113.
Poem.

C119 THOSE WERE THE DAYS. *Canadian Forum*, XLI, 487 (August 1961), 113.
Poem.

C120 BE PATIENT FOR THE WOLF. *X:A Quarterly Review*, London, II, 2 (August 1961), 85–86.
Poem.

C121 HEBEPHRENE'S STEEP. *X:A Quarterly Review*, II, 2 (August 1961), 86–87.
Poem.

C122 DELIRIUM IN VERA CRUZ. *X:A Quarterly Review*, II, 2 (August 1961), 87.
Poem.

C123 READING DON QUIXOTE. *X:A Quarterly Review*, II, 2 (August 1961), 87.
Poem.

C124 QUEER POEM. *The New York Times*, CX, 37, 827 (17 September 1961), section 4, p. 10E.
Poem.

C125 PREFACE TO A NOVEL. *Canadian Literature*, no. 9 (Summer 1961), 23–29.
A translation into English, by George Woodcock, of Lowry's preface to the French edition of *Under the Volcano.* The note preceding the preface states that it "was prepared while Malcolm Lowry was working with Clarisse Françillon on her translation of his novel; the final version was actually prepared in French from Lowry's English notes, so that no English original exists."

C126 THE UNBORN. *Virginia Quarterly Review*, Charlottesville, XXXVII, 3 (Summer 1961), 396.
Poem.

C127 THERE IS A METALLURGY. *Virginia Quarterly Review*, XXXVII, 3 (Summer 1961), 397.
Poem.

C128 POETS ARE GODLIKE. *Virginia Quarterly Review*, XXXVII, 3 (Summer 1961), 397.
Poem.

C129 COMFORT. *Paris Review*, no. 26 (Summer/Fall 1961), 28.
Poem.

C130 MERCY OF FIRE. *Paris Review,* no. 26 (Summer/Fall 1961), 28.
Poem.

C131 DEATH OF A OAXAQUENIAN. *Paris Review*, no. 26 (Summer/Fall 1961), 29.
Poem.

C132 FROM HELSINKI TO LIVERPOOL WITH LUMBER. *Review of English Literature,* London, II, 4 (October 1961), 37.
Poem.

C133 [A marathon of gulls.] *Harper's Bazaar*, New York, no. 3,000 (November 1961), 181.
Untitled poem.

C134 IT WAS NOT SO. *Harper's Bazaar*, no. 3,000 (November 1961), 181.
Poem.

C135 NO KRAKEN SHALL BE FOUND TILL SOUGHT BY NAME. *American Scholar*, Washington, XXX, 4 (Autumn 1961), 530.
Poem.

C136 FOUL ACAPULCO. *Carleton Miscellany,* Northfield, Minn., II, 4 (Fall 1961), 34.
Poem.

C137 YOU THINK YOU ARE A MAN. *Carleton Miscellany,* II, 4 (Fall 1961), 34–35.
Poem.

C138 HYPOCRITE! OXFORD GROUPER! YAHOO! *Carleton Miscellany*, II, 4 (Fall 1961), 35.
Poem.

C139 QUARTERMASTER AT THE WHEEL. *The Dalhousie Review*, Halifax, XLI, 3 (Autumn 1961), 383.
Poem.

C140 [THIS BITTEREST COAST.] *The Dalhousie Review*, XLI, 3 (Autumn 1961), 384.
Poem.

C141 [THIS DEAD LETTER.] *The Dalhousie Review*, XLI, 3 (Autumn 1961), 384–385.
Poem.

C142 [WHIRLPOOL.] *The Dalhousie Review*, XLI, 3 (Autumn 1961), 385.
Poem. Reprinted, slightly revised, in *Selected Poems.*

C143 SOME SWORD FOR ME. *Epoch*, Ithaca, N.Y., XI, 3 (Fall 1961), 157.
Poem.

C144 ONE FLYING LINE. *Epoch*, XI, 3 (Fall 1961), 157–158.
Poem.

C145 CORRECTING MANUSCRIPT. *Epoch*, XI, 3 (Fall 1961), 158.
Poem.

C146 ON READING MELVILLE'S REDBURN. *Epoch*, XI, 3 (Fall 1961), 158.
Poem.

C147 INJURED CHORIANT OR PAEONIC. *Epoch*, XI, 3 (Fall 1961), 159.
Poem.

C148 THIRTY-FIVE MESCALS IN CUAUTLA. *The Minnesota Review*, Minneapolis, II, 1 (Fall 1961), 24–25.
Poem.

C149 WALK IN CANADA. *Queen's Quarterly*, Toronto, LXVIII, 3 (Autumn 1961), 418–419.
Poem.

C150 THE WESTERN OCEAN. *Queen's Quarterly*, LXVIII, 3 (Autumn 1961), 420.
Poem.

C151 THE WILD CHERRY. *Queen's Quarterly*, LXVIII, 3 (Autumn 1961), 420.
Poem.

C152 VENUS. *Western Humanities Review*, Salt Lake City, XV, 4 (Autumn 1961), 332.
Poem.

C153 LIFE IN DEATH. *Western Humanities Review*, XV, 4 (Autumn 1961), 333.
Poem.

C154 LOOK OUT! THE BLOODY BOSUN! *London Magazine*, I, 9 (December 1961), 27.
Poem.

C155 BYZANTIUM. *London Magazine*, I, 9 (December 1961), 27.
Poem.

C156 VISITING THE WRECK: AN ABLE SEAMAN EXPLAINS. *London Magazine*, I, 9 (December 1961), 28.
Poem.

C157 NO COMPANY BUT FEAR. *Arizona Quarterly*, Tucson, XVII, 4 (Winter 1961), 360.
Poem.

1962

C158 THE EX-POET. *Saturday Review*, New York, 6 January 1962, 21.
Poem.

C159 THOUGHTS WHILE DROWNING. *Audience*, Cambridge, Mass., VIII, 3 (January 1962), 42.
Poem. Reprinted, slightly revised, in *Selected Poems.*

C160 THE LIGHTHOUSE INVITES THE STORM. *Audience*, VIII, 3 (January 1962), 43.
Poem.

C161 IN THE SHED. *Delta*, Montreal, no. 17 (January 1962), 9.
Poem.

C162 LOATHING. *Delta,* no. 17 (January 1962), 9.
Poem.

C163 ON READING EDMUND WILSON'S REMARKS ABOUT RIMBAUD. *Delta*, no. 17 (January 1962), 10.
Poem.

C164 QUATRAINS. *Delta,* no. 17 (January 1962), 11.
Poem.

C165 MEN WITH COATS THRASHING. *Exchange*, Montreal, II. 3 (February/March 1962), 10.
Poem.

C166 FOUL OR TWENTY-FIVE! *Raven*, Vancouver, no. 10 (March 1962), 5.
Poem.

C167 THE SUN WAS ALMOST SHINING. *Raven*, no. 10 (March 1962), 6.
Poem.

C168 FOR UNDER THE VOLCANO. *Evidence*, Toronto, no. 4 (Winter 1962), 81–82.
Poem. The version in *Selected Poems* is slightly revised.

C169 SELF PITY. *Evidence*, no. 4 (Winter 1962), 82.
Poem.

C170 PRAYER (FOR HIS FATHER). *Evidence*, no. 4 (Winter 1962), 83.
Poem.

C171 RILKE AND YEATS. *Evidence*, no. 4 (Winter 1962), 83.
Poem.

C172 DOCTOR USQUEBAUGH. *Evidence*, no. 4 (Winter 1962), 84.
Poem.

C173 HUNGER. *Northwest Review*, Eugene, Oregon, V, 1 (Winter 1962), 60.
Poem.

C174 IRON CITIES. *Northwest Review*, V, 1 (Winter 1962), 61.
Poem.

C175 THE DOOMED IN THEIR SINKING. *Northwest Review*, V, 1 (Winter 1962), 62.
Poem.

C176 THE SHIP IS TURNING HOMEWARD. *Northwest Review*, V, 1 (Winter 1962), 63.
Poem. Reprinted, with revisions, in *Selected Poems.*

C177 S. S. HOUSMAN. *Northwest Review*, V, 1 (Winter 1962), 64.
Poem.

C178 AT THE BAR. *Northwest Review*, V, 1 (Winter 1962), 64.
Poem.

C179 SUNRISE. *Northwest Review*, V, 1 (Winter 1962), 65.
Poem, reprinted from C48 with several corrections and several typographical errors.

C180 WIND BLOWING THROUGH THE SHACK. *Northwest Review*, V, 1 (Winter 1962), 66.
Poem.

C181 THE WOUNDED BAT. *Northwest Review*, V, 1 (Winter 1962), 66.
Poem.

C182 EELS. *Northwest Review*, V, 1 (Winter 1962), 67.
Poem.

C183 FRAGMENT II. *Northwest Review*, V, 1 (Winter 1962), 68.
Unfinished poem beginning, "When I was young I broke all drinking records."

C184 HANGOVER—READING RILKE, SCHNITZLER OR SOMEONE. *Northwest Review*, V, 1 (Winter 1962), 69.
Poem.

C185 THE DRUNKARDS. *The New Yorker*, XXXVIII, 11 (5 May 1962), 46.
Two sonnets, both reprinted in *Selected Poems*; the first, beginning "Notions of freedom are tied up with drink" under the title "Without the Nighted Wyvern" and the second, beginning "The noise of death is in this desolate bar" as "The Drunkards."

C186 KINGFISHERS IN BRITISH COLUMBIA. *The Atlantic Monthly*, CCIX, 6 (June 1962), 55.
Poem.

C187 LETTER FROM LOWRY. *Canadian Forum*, XLII, 497 (June 1962), 62–63.
Shortened version of a letter to Derek Pethick on the influence of *Moby Dick* on *Under the Volcano*. Published in full in *Selected Letters*.

C188 HAPPINESS. *Ladies Home Journal*, Philadelphia, LXXIX, 6 (June 1962), 88.
Poem.

C189 POEM. *The Fiddlehead*, Fredericton, N.B., no. 52 (Spring 1962), 8.
Untitled poem, beginning "Like the black iron steps." Reprinted in *Selected Poems* under the title "A New Ship."

C190 THE COILED HEART. *The Fiddlehead*, no. 52 (Spring 1962), 8.
Poem.

C191 THE SHIP OF WAR. *The Fiddlehead*, no. 52 (Spring 1962), 9.
Poem.

C192 LOVE WHICH COMES TOO LATE. *Perspective*, St. Louis, XII, 4 (Spring 1962), 172.
Poem.

C193 INJURED STONES. *Perspective*, XII, 4 (Spring 1962), 172.
Poem.

C194 [SAINT MALCOLM AMONG THE BIRDS.] *Tamarack Review*, no. 23 (Spring 1962), 39.
Poem.

C195 [HE LIKED THE DEAD.] *Tamarack Review*, no. 23 (Spring 1962), 40.
Poem.

C196 EPITAPH. *Tamarack Review*, no. 23 (Spring 1962), 40.
Poem.

C197 FOR THE LOVE OF DYING. *Harper's Magazine*, New York, CCXXV, 1348 (September 1962), 38.
Poem.

C198 THUNDER BEYOND POPOCATÉPETL. *Southwest Review*, Dallas, XLVII, 3 (Summer 1962), 230.
Poem.

1963

C199 LUNAR CAUSTIC. *Paris Review*, no. 29 (Winter/Spring 1963), 15–72.

Short story. First English version, edited by Earle Birney and Margerie Lowry; preceded by an earlier version in French published in *Esprit* (D21). This English version was subsequently translated into French and published in *Les lettres nouvelles* (D24). See A8*an* for a history of this title.

C200 UNDER THE VOLCANO. *Prairie Schooner*, Lincoln, Nebraska, XXXVII, 4 (Winter 1963/64), 284–300.
Short story; first version of what was later developed into chapter VIII of the novel *Under the Volcano.*

C201 THREE UNPUBLISHED LETTERS. *Prairie Schooner*, XXXVII, 4 (Winter 1963/64), 321–327.
Letters to John Davenport, Nordahl Grieg, and Downie Kirk, all reprinted in *Selected Letters.*

C202 AGAINST THE SPELL OF DEATH by Earle Birney. *Prairie Schooner*, XXXVII, 4 (Winter 1963/64), 328–333.
Quotes from the poems "Note for a poem," "Reading Don Quixote," "Love which comes too late," "Reflection to windward," and "To three in London," as well as from several poems already collected in *Selected Poems.*

C203 PRAYER FROM THE WICKET GATE FOR FORTY ONE DOORS FOR FORTY TWO, *Prairie Schooner*, XXXVII, 4 (Winter 1963/64), 333–334.
Poem. First published in French translation in *Les lettres nouvelles* (July/August 1960) (D22). Written as a sonnet for New Year's Day 1942 to Conrad Aiken, who called his home at Brewster, Mass., "Forty-One Doors." Lowry had named his Dollarton beach shack "The Wicket Gate."

C204 ON BOARD THE *MATSUE MARU. Prairie Schooner*, XXXVII, 4 (Winter 1963/64), 334.
Poem.

C205 [THE SUN SHINES.] *Prairie Schooner*, XXXVII, 4 (Winter 1963/64), 334.
Poem.

C206 [WRECKER OF GARDENS.] *Prairie Schooner*, XXXVII, 4 (Winter 1963/64), 335.
Poem.

1964

C207 THE ELEMENT FOLLOWS YOU AROUND, SIR! *Show Magazine*, New York, IV, 3 (March 1964), 45.
Short story. Revised to become chapter 18 of *October Ferry to Gabriola.*

C208 MALCOLM LOWRY: LETTERS TO AN EDITOR by Douglas Day. *Shenandoah*, Lexington, Va., XV, 3 (Spring 1964), 3–15.
Contains excerpts from Lowry's letters to his editor, Albert Erskine, later published in full in *Selected Letters.*

1965

C209 BULLS OF THE RESURRECTION. *Prism International*, Vancouver, V, 1 (Summer 1965), 4–11.
Short story.

C210 EXPLICATION OF RICHARD EBERHART'S "CARAVAN OF SILENCE." House of Books, Ltd., New York, undated catalogue (ca. November 1965), item 381.
Quotes a note sending John Davenport a two page explication of Eberhart's poem, ca. 1930.

C211 LES OEUVRES DE JEUNESSE DE MALCOLM LOWRY by Suzanne Kim. *Etudes Anglaises*, Paris, XVIIIe annee, 4 (October/December 1965), 383–394.
Reprints, in English, the poem "Number 8 Fireman" from *The Leys Fortnightly* of 1 June 1928 (C24).

1966

C212 MALCOLM LOWRY: A REMINISCENCE by David Markson. *Nation*, New York, CCII, 16 (7 February 1966), 164–167.
Contains the text of a telegram Lowry sent to Conrad Aiken in 1954. Not in *Selected Letters.*

1967

C213 MALCOLM LOWRY A FIRST IMPRESSION by James Stern. *Encounter*, London, XXIX, 3 (September 1967), 58–68.
Prints the text of a postcard sent by Lowry to Stern in early 1947. Not in *Selected Letters.*

1968

C214 CONVERSATIONS WITH GOETHE. *A Malcolm Lowry Catalogue* edited by J. Howard Woolmer. Focus Series no. 2, New York, 1968, 12.
Poem.

C215 REFLECTION TO WINDWARD. *A Malcolm Lowry Catalogue* edited by J. Howard Woolmer. Focus Series no. 2, 1968, 13.
Poem.

1970

C216 LETTER TO ALBERT ERSKINE. *Canadian Literature*, no. 44 (Spring 1970), 50–52.
Letter (Dollarton, 1946), beginning "Dear Mr. Erskine: Well every man has his own Laocoon . . ." Not included in *Selected Letters.*

C217 LETTER TO DAVID MARKSON. *Canadian Literature*, no. 44 (Spring 1970), 53–56.
Letter (Dollarton, 20 June 1951), beginning "Dear David Markson: I thank you sincerely for your letter . . ." Not included in *Selected Letters.*

C218 MALCOLM LOWRY AND THE CINEMA by Paul G. Tiessen. *Canadian Literature*, no. 44 (Spring 1970), 38–49.
Contains quotations from an unpublished letter of 31 October 1951 to Clemens ten Holder; from Lowry's film treatment of "The Bravest Boat," (see note following); and from his film treatment of F. Scott Fitzgerald's *Tender Is the Night.* In the *Malcolm Lowry Newsletter*, no. 4 (Spring 1979), 17, Tiessen states that he now doubts that Lowry ever wrote a film-script of "The Bravest Boat." The script was in fact written by Robert D. Graff in the early 1960s, but it was never produced.

1973

C219 GHOSTKEEPER. *American Review*, New York, no. 17 (May 1973), 1–34.
Short story.

1974

C220 A FEW ITEMS CULLED FROM WHAT STARTED OUT TO BE A SORT OF PREFACE TO A FILM SCRIPT by Malcolm and Margerie Lowry. With introduction and notes by Paul Tiessen. *White Pelican*, Edmonton, IV, 2 (Spring 1974), 2–20.
This "preface" to the Lowrys' treatment of F. Scott Fitzgerald's *Tender Is the Night* takes the form of a letter to Frank Taylor. Tiessen's introduction quotes from an earlier version. Not in *Selected Letters*, but see Lowry's letter to Frank Taylor dated 12 April 1950 in that volume.

1976

C221 Letters to John Davenport. Sotheby & Co. (Hodgson's Rooms) catalogue for the sale of 17 December 1976 (lot 611) has several minor quotes from a series of letters from Lowry to Davenport.

1980

C222 NOTES FOR *DARK AS THE GRAVE WHEREIN MY FRIEND IS LAID*. Glenn Horowitz, Bookseller, New York, catalogue 3 (ca. November 1980), item 193.
Quotes from Lowry's 43 pages of holograph notes for this book. Also included in this catalogue is the manuscript of an unpublished and untitled poem (item 190); the surviving 16 pages of typescript of the novel *In Ballast to the White Sea* (item 191); the four-page typescript of a short story "Way Down Yonder in New Orleans" (item 192); and a fifty-one-page typescript "Material mostly for Eridanus" (item 194). All of these, with the exception of item 193, are repeated in Horowitz' catalogue 5 (ca. March 1982).
Eridanus, Lowry's name for Dollarton, was a projected novella later largely incorporated into *October Ferry to Gabriola*.

1981

C223 HAITIAN NOTEBOOK. Glenn Horowitz, Bookseller, New York, catalogue 4 (ca. May 1981), item 408.
Quotes from a 60-page pocket-size notebook kept by Lowry on his trip to Haiti in 1946. This item is repeated in Horowitz' catalogue 5 (ca. March 1982).

C224 LAST NOTEBOOK. Glenn Horowitz, New York, catalogue 4 (ca. May 1981), item 409.
Quotes from a half-used 40-page notebook carried by Lowry on a walking tour of the Lake District in 1957. This item is repeated in Horowitz' catalogue 5 (ca. March 1982).

SECTION D
Translations

D. Translations

CATALÁN

BOOKS:

D1 *Soto el volcá.* [*Under the Volcano.*]. Translated by Manuel de Pedrolo. Barcelona: Edicions 62, (1973).

DANISH

BOOKS:

D2 *Under vulkanen.* [*Under the Volcano.*] Translated by Vibeke Bloch. Kobenhaven: Gyldendal, 1949. Reprinted 1968.

DUTCH

BOOKS:

D3 *Onder de vulkaan.* [*Under the Volcano.*] Translated by John Vandenbergh. Amsterdam: Uitgeverij de Bezige Bij, 1966. Reprinted 1971.

ANTHOLOGIES:

D3α *De beste buitenlandse verhalen van de Bezige Bij.* Amsterdam: Uitgeverij de Bezige Bij, 1978.
Contains Jan Gerhard Toonder's translation of "Present Estate of Pompeii," ("De huidige staat van Pompeji"), 127.

FINNISH

BOOKS:

D4 *Tulivuoren juurella.* [*Under the Volcano.*]. Translated by Juhani Jaskari. Helsinki: Werner Soderstram Osakeyhtio, 1968.

FRENCH

BOOKS:

D5 *Au-dessous du volcan.* [*Under the Volcano.*] Translated by Stephen Spriel with the collaboration of Clarisse Francillon and the author. Preface by Malcolm Lowry; postface by Max-Pol Fouchet. Paris: Le Club français du livre, 1949. Limitations as follows: 1,000 copies numbered 1 to 1,000 reserved for "promoteurs de l'édition"; 26 copies lettered A to Z and 100 copies numbered I to C for "animateurs du Club"; and 3,000 copies numbered 1,001 to 4,000.

D6 *Au-dessous du volcan.* Paris: Correa, 1950. Reprint of D5. Also a limited edition of 50 numbered copies on vélin supérior.

D7 *Au-dessous du volcan.* New edition with avant-propos by Maurice Nadeau. Paris: Le Club français du livre, 1959. Limited to 26 copies lettered A to Z, 100 copies numbered I to C, and 7,000 copies numbered 1 to 7,000.

D8 *Au-dessous du volcan.* Paris: Correa, 1960. Reprint of D7.

D9 *Au-dessous du volcan.* Edition définitive entièrement revue et corrigée. Translated by Stephen Spriel with the collaboration of Clarisse Francillon. Avant-propos de Maurice Nadeau; postface de Max-Pol Fouchet. Paris: Buchet/Chastel, 1960. Reprinted 1963, 1966, 1969.

D10 *Au-dessous du volcan.* Paris: Le Club français du livre, 1971. Reprint of D9.

D11 *Au-dessous du volcan.* Paris: Gallimard, 1973. Reprint of D9. Reissued 1978.

D12 *Ultramarine.* Translated by Clarisse Francillon and Jean-Roger Carroy. Dirigée par Maurice Nadeau; postface par Jean-Roger Carroy. Paris: Les lettres nouvelles, Denöel, 1965.

D13 *Sombre comme la tombe òu repose mon ami.* [*Dark as the Grave Wherein My Friend Is Laid.*] Translated by Clarisse Francillon. Paris: Les lettres nouvelles, Denöel, 1970.

D14 *Choix de lettres.* [*Selected Letters*, abridged.] Translated by Suzanne Kim. Paris: Denöel, (1968). Issued with a wrap-around band.

D15 *En route vers l'île de Gabriola.* [*October Ferry to Gabriola.*] Translated by Clarisse Francillon. Paris: Les lettres nouvelles, Denöel, 1972.

D16 *Pour l'amour de mourir.* [*Selected Poems.*] Gouaches découpées de Júlio Pomar. Translated by J.-M. Lucchioni. Preface by Bernard Noel. (Paris), Editions de la difference, Collection le milieu, (1976). Also issued in a limited edition of 62 copies with an original lithograph signed, numbered I to XII and 1 to 50. Contains "No kraken shall be found till sought by name," ("Nul ne trouve le kraken s'il ne le cherche sous son vrai nom"), "Look out! The bloody bosun," ("Fais gaffe! V'la ce salaud de quartier-maitre!"), "Byzantium," ("Byzance"), "Old freighter in an old port," ("Dans un vieux port, un vieux cargo"), "Iron cities," ("Villes de fer"), "The flowering past," ("Quand le passé fleurit"), "The ship is turning homeward," ("Le chemin du retour"), "The lighthouse invites the storm," ("Le phare attire la tempête"), "Tashtego believed red," ("Tashtego croyait au rouge"), "Vigil Forget," "The days like smitten cymbals of brass," ("Jours pareils à des cymbales de bronze"), "Thunder beyond Popocatepetl," ("Tonnerre derrière le Popocatepetl"), "For *Under the Volcano,*" ("Pour Au-dessous de volcan"), "Xochitepec," "The volcano is dark," ("Le volcan est sombre"), "Grim vinegarroon," ("Le scorpion tenace"), "In the Oaxaca jail," ("Dans la prison d'Oaxaca"), "For the love of dying," ("Pour l'amour de mourir"), "Death of a Oaxaquenian," ("Mort d'un habitant d'Oaxaca"), "In a Mexican church," ("Dans une église Mexicaine"), "Delirium in Vera Cruz," ("Délire a Véra Cruz"), "Sunrise," ("Lever de soleil"), "Prayer for drunks," ("Prière pour les ivrognes"), "Thirty-five mescals in Cuautla," ("Trente-cinq mescals a Cuantla" *sic*), "Eye-opener," ("De quoi vous ouvrir les yeux"), "No company but fear," ("Seul avec la peur"), "No time to stop and think," ("Pas le temps de s'arrêter pour réfléchir"), "Comfort," ("Réconfort"), "Without the nighted wyvern," ("Sans la guivre dans la nuit"), "The drunkards," ("Les ivrognes"), "At the bar," ("Au bar"), "Sestina in a cantina," ("Sestina dans une cantina"), "Venus," "Fragment," "A new ship," ("Un nouveau navire"), "A poem of God's mercy," ("Poème sur la miséricorde divine"), "A quarrel," ("Une dispute"), "No still path," ("Aucun chemin tranquille"), "Nocturne," "Saint Malcolm among the birds," ("Saint Malcolm parmi les oiseaux"), "Happiness," ("Bonheur"), "Hostage," ("Otage"), "Be patient for the wolf," ("Sois patient, car le loup"), "The comedian," ("Le comique"), "Men with coats thrashing," ("Des hommes dont le vent fait claquer le pardessus"), "Thoughts while drowning," ("Pensées d'un homme qui se noie"), "Queer poem," ("Poème bizarre"), "Poem," ("Poème"), "Midtown pyromaniac," ("Le pyromane du centre-ville"), "Injured stones," ("Pierres blessées"), "Kingfishers in British Columbia," ("Martins-pêcheurs en Colombie Britannique"), "Christ walks in this infernal district too," ("Le Christ visite aussi ces quartiers infernaux"), "Whirlpool," ("Tourbillon"), "The glaucous-winged gull," ("La mouette aux ailes glauques"), "The ship sails on: For Nordahl Grieg," ("Le navire continue son voyage pour Nordahl Grieg"), "The wounded bat," ("Le chauve-souris blessée"), "The past," ("Le passé"), "The pilgrim," ("Le pèlerin"), "The wild cherry," ("Le cerisier sauvage"), "Rilke and Yeats," ("Rilke et Yeats"), "Thoughts to be erased from my destiny," ("Pensées a effacer de mon destin"), "Joseph Conrad," "Trinity," ("Trinité"), "The doomed in their sinking," ("Les naufragés au moment de couler"), "Eels," ("Les anguilles"), "The plagiarist," ("Le plagiaire"), "He liked the dead," ("Il aimait bien les morts"), "The search," ("La quête"), "After publication of *Under the Volcano*," ("Le succès"), "Strange type," ("Une impression bizarre").

D17 *Lunar Caustic*, revised translation by Clarisse Francillon. *Le caustique lunaire*, translated by Michele d'Astorg and Clarisse Francillon; definitive version by Clarisse Francillon. Preface by Maurice Nadeau. Paris: Les lettres nouvelles/Maurice Nadeau, 1977. The two French versions in one volume. See A8*an* for a history of this title.

PERIODICALS:

D18 *Mercure de France*, Paris, no. 1034 (1 October 1949), 271.
Contains a translation by Stephen Rorce, assisted by Clarisse Francillon, with the collaboration of the author, of the first chapter of *Under the Volcano*, (*Au-dessous du volcan*). Rorce was subsequently replaced as translator by Stephen Spriel.

D19 *Les lettres nouvelles*, Paris (November 1953), 1067.
Contains a translation of "The Bravest Boat," ("Brave petit bateau"), by Georges Belmont. Reprinted in D23.

D20 *Les lettres nouvelles* (September 1955), 193.
Contains a translation by Roger Giroux of "Strange Comfort Afforded by the Profession," ("Étrange réconfort").

D21 *Esprit*, Paris (February, March & April 1956), 211; 341; 525.
Contains a translation by Michele d'Astorg and Clarisse Francillon of *Lunar Caustic*, (*Le caustique lunaire*). Serialized in the three issues. See A8*an* for a history of this title.

D22 *Les lettres nouvelles* (July/August 1960).
Contains translations of the short stories "Present Estate of Pompeii," ("Pompei, aujourd'hui") 26, and "Through the Panama" ("La Traversée du Panama") 109, by Clarisse Francillon; translations of the poems "Mr. Lowry's derivative Good Friday under a real cactus," ("Le vendredi-saint de M. Lowry sous un véritable cactus"), "Eye-opener," ("Réveil"), "Harpies," "The flowering past," ("Nulle poésie"), "No time to stop and think," ("Pas le temps de s'arrêter ni réfléchir"), "Men with coats thrashing," ("Hommes a vestes battantes"), "Prayer from the Wicket Gate for Forty One Doors for forty two," ("Prière pour l'année

nouvelle"), and "Stoker Tom's ukelele," ("L'ukulele de Tom le chauffeur") 89, by Jean Follain; and translations by Clarisse Francillon of ten letters from Lowry, five to Albert Erskine, four to David Markson, and one to Clarisse Francillon, 184. One of the letters to Erskine (15 July 1946) and the letter to Francillon have not been published in English; one of the letters to Markson (ca. 24 May 1954) does not appear in *Selected Letters* but was published in *Canadian Literature* no. 8 (C92). Also contains a reproduction of an unidentified page of Lowry manuscript, 82.

Note: See D30 for a revision of Follain's translation of "Men with coats thrashing," and "No time to stop and think."

D23 *Les lettres nouvelles* (July/August 1962), whole issue.
Contains a translation by Clarisse Francillon (with the exception of "The Bravest Boat," which was translated by Georges Belmont) of *Hear us O Lord from heaven thy dwelling place* (*Ecoute notre voix ô Seigneur*). The Belmont translation is reprinted from D19.

D24 *Les lettres nouvelles* (April 1963), whole issue.
Contains a translation by Clarisse Francillon of *Lunar Caustic.* See A8*an* for a history of this title.

D25 *Les lettres nouvelles* (February/March 1964), 5.
Contains a translation by Genevieve Serreau and Robert Pepin of "Garden of Etla," ("Le Jardin d'Etla").

D26 *Les lettres nouvelles* (November/December 1964), 5.
Contains a translation by Clarisse Francillon and Genevieve Serreau of "The Element Follows You Around, Sir!" ("Le feu de ciel vous suit à la trace, Monsieur!").

D27 *Les lettres nouvelles* (May/June 1968), 11.
Contains a translation by Suzanne Kim of Lowry's 2 January 1946 letter to Jonathan Cape about *Under the Volcano* ("Tentative d'explication d'au -dessous du volcan").

D28 *Les lettres nouvelles* (May/June 1970), 86.
Contains a translation by Serge Fauchereau of the poem "Reading Don Quixote," ("Don Quichotte").

D29 *Les lettres nouvelles* (May/June 1972), 63.
Contains a translation by Clarisse Francillon of chapter 31, "Twilight of the Raven," from *October Ferry to Gabriola*, ("Crépuscule du corbeau").

D30 *Les lettres nouvelles* (May/June 1974), special Malcolm Lowry issue.
Contains the poem "Cain shall not slay Abel today on our good ground," ("Cain ne tuera pas Abel sur notre bonne terre"), translated by R. I. Yacoubovitch, and the following poems, all translated by Jean Follain, "No kraken shall be found till sought by name," ("On ne trouve un 'Kraken' qui si l'on en sait le nom"), "Xochitepec," "In the Oaxaca gaol," ("Dans la prison d'Oaxaca"), "Delirium in Vera Cruz," ("Divagation a Veracruz"), "Thirty-five mescals in Cuautla," ("Trente-cinq mescals a Cuautla"), "No company but fear," ("Pas de compagnie hormis la peur"), "No time to stop and think," ("Pas le temps de s'arreter ni reflechir"); "Without the nighted wyvern," ("Sans le dragon nocturne"), "Fragment," "No still path," ("Point de sentier tranquille"), "Epitaph," ("Epitaphe"), "Rilke and Yeats," ("Rilke et Yeats"), "Men with coats thrashing," ("Hommes a vetements claquants"), "Poem 'Wet streets in Liverpool'," ("Poeme"), "Thoughts to be erased from my destiny," ("Pensees a effacer de mon destin"), and "After publication of 'Under the Volcano'," ("Apres la parution de 'Au-dessous du volcan' "), 221; and six letters from Lowry to Jonathan Cape, Mr. Clark, Albert Erskine, Mr. Neeves, Gerald Noxon (2), 241; only the Erskine letter, which is misdated, appeared in *Selected Letters.*

Note: The translation of "Men with coats thrashing" and "No time to stop and think" are revisions of Follain's translations in D22.

D31 *La nouvelle revue française*, Paris (January 1979), 156.
Contains the following poems in English, and in French translation by Madelaine and Jean Follain: "In a Mexican church," ("Dans une église Mexicaine"), "Trinity," ("Trinité"), "Christ walks in this infernal district too," ("Le Christ chemine aussi dans cet infernal quartier"), "A new ship," ("Un bateau neuf"), "Happiness," ("Bonheur"), "Nocturne", and "The glaucous-winged gull," ("Le goéland aux ailes glauques").

GERMAN

BOOKS:

D32 *Unter dem Vulkan.* [*Under the Volcano.*] Translated by Clemens ten Holder. Stuttgart: Ernst Klett, (1951). Issued in dust jacket.

D33 *Unter dem Vulkan.* [*Under the Volcano.*]. Translated by Susanne Rademacher. Hamburg: Rowohlt, 1963. Issued in dust jacket. Reissued in 1974.

D34 *Hors uns, o Herr, der Du im Himmel wohnst.* [*Hear us O Lord from heaven thy dwelling place.*] Translated by Susanne Rademacher. Hamburg: Rowohlt, 1965. Issued in dust jacket.

D35 *Die letzte adresse.* [*Lunar Caustic.*] Translated by Martin Kluger. Frankfurt: Suhrkamp Verlag, 1977.

D36 *Oktoberfahre nach Gabriola.* [*October Ferry to Gabriola*]. Translated by Susanne Rademacher. Foreword by Wolf Wondratschek. Hamburg: Rowohlt, 1981. First volume of a proposed eight-volume "Collected Works of Malcolm Lowry," edited by Christa Cooper and Joachim Sartorius.

D36α *Ultramarin.* [*Ultramarine.*] Translated by Werner Schmitz. Hamburg: Rowohlt, 1982. Second volume of a proposed eight-volume "Collected Works of Malcolm Lowry," edited by Christa Cooper and Joachim Sartorius.

GREEK

BOOKS:

D37 *To Monopati tes Bruses.* ["The Forest Path to the Spring."] Translated by Strate Tsirka. Athens: Ekdoseis "Kedros," 1968.

HUNGARIAN

BOOKS:

D38 *Vulkán Alatt.* [*Under the Volcano.*] Translated by Árpád Göncz. Budapest: Europa Konyvkiado, 1973. Issued in dust jacket.

D39 *At a Panamán. Elefánt és kolosszeum. A forráshoz vezetö erdei ösvény.* ["Through the Panama," "Elephant and Colosseum," and "The Forest Path to the Spring."] Translated by Árpád Göncz. Budapest: Europa Konyvkiado, 1974.

ITALIAN

BOOKS:

D40 *Sotto il vulcano.* [*Under the Volcano.*] Translated by Giorgio Monicelli. Milan; Feltrinelli, 1961. Issued in dust jacket. Reissued in 1966.

D41 *Ultramarina.* [*Ultramarine.*] Translated by Valerio Riva. Milan: Feltrinelli, 1963. Issued in dust jacket.

D42 *Ascoltaci, Signore.* [*Hear us O Lord from heaven thy dwelling place.*] Translated by Attilio Veraldi. Milan: Feltrinelli, 1969. Issued in dust jacket.

D43 *Buio come la tomba dove giace il mio amico.* [*Dark as the Grave Wherein My Friend Is Laid.*] Translated by Attilio Veraldi. Milan: Arnoldo Mondadori, 1971.

D44 *L'urlo del mare e il buio.* [*Selected Poems.*] Translated and with a preface by Francesco Vizioli. Parma: Guanda Editore, 1972. English and Italian text. Contains Earle Birney's introduction from A5.

Contains "No kraken shall be found till sought by name," ("Non troveremo i mostri se non chiamandoli per nome"), "Look out! The bloody bosun," ("Attenti, c'è il maledetto nostromo"), "Byzantium," ("Bisanzio"), "Old freighter in an old port," ("Vecchia nave in vecchio porto"), "Iron cities," ("Le città di ferro"), "The flowering past," ("Il passato in fiore"), "The ship is turning homeward," ("La nave volge la prua verso casa"), "The lighthouse invites the storm," ("Il faro invita la tempesta"), "Tashtego believed red," ("Tashtego creduto rosso"), "Vigil Forget," "The days like smitten cymbals of brass," ("I giorni come suoni di piatti di ottone"), "Thunder beyond Popocatepetl," ("Il tuorno dietro il Popocatepetl"), "For 'Under the Volcano'," ("Per 'Sotto il vulcano' "), "Xochitepec," "The volcano is dark," ("Il vulcano è scuro"), "Grim vinegarroon," ("Lo scorpione velenoso"), "In the Oaxaca Jail," ("Nella prigione di Oaxaca"), "For the love of dying," ("Per amor di morire"), "Death of a Oaxaquenian," ("Morte di un Oaxaqueniano"), "In a Mexican church," ("In una chiesa Messicana"), "Delirium in Vera Cruz," ("Delerio a Vera Cruz"), "Sunrise," ("Il sorgere del sole"), "Prayer for drunks," ("Preghiera per gli ubriachi"), "Thirty-five mescals in Cuautla," ("Trentacinque mescal a

Cuautla"), "Eye-opener," ("Apriocchi"), "No company but fear," ("Sola compagna la paura"), "No time to stop and think," ("Non c'è tempo per fermarsi a pensare"), "Comfort," ("Conforto"), "Without the nighted wyvern," ("Senza il drago della notte"), "The drunkards," ("Gli ubriachi"), "At the bar," ("Al bar"), "Venus," ("Venere"), "Fragment," ("Frammento"), "A new ship," ("Una nave nuova"), "A poem of God's mercy," ("Poema per la divina misericordia"), "A quarrel," ("Una lite"), "No still path," ("Nessun sentiero silenzioso"), "Nocturne," ("Notturno"), "Saint Malcolm among the birds," ("San Malcolm tra gli uccelli"), "Happiness," ("Felicità"), "Be patient for the wolf," ("Pazienta, perché il lupo"), "The comedian," ("Il commediante"), "Men with coats thrashing," ("Uomini dagli abiti sbattuti"), "Thoughts while drowning," ("Pensieri mentre si annega"), "Queer poem," ("Poesia strana"), "Poem," ("Poesia"), "Midtown pyromaniac," ("Il piromane urbano"), "Injured stones," ("Pietre ferite"), "Epitaph," ("Epitaffio"), "Kingfishers in British Columbia," ("Martin pescatori nella Columbia Britannica"), "Christ walks in this infernal district too," ("Cristo passa anche da questo infernale quartiere"), "Whirlpool," ("Gorgo"), "Hostage," ("Ostaggio"), "The glaucous-winged gull," ("Il gabbiano con le ali azzurre"), "The ship sails on: For Nordahl Grieg," ("La nave salpa: per Nordahl Grieg"), "The wounded bat," ("Il pipistrello ferito"), "The past," ("Il passato"), "The pilgrim," ("Il pellegrino"), "The wild cherry," ("Il ciliegio selvatico"), "Rilke and Yeats," ("Rilke e Yeats"), "Thoughts to be erased from my destiny," ("Pensieri da cancellare dal mio destino"), "Joseph Conrad," "Trinity," ("Trinità"), "The Doomed in their sinking," ("I condannati che affogano"), "Eels," ("Le anguille"), "The plagiarist [fragment]," ("Il plagiario [frammento]"), "He liked the dead," ("Egli amava le cose morte"), "After publication of 'Under the Volcano'," ("Dopo la pubblicazione di 'Sotto il vulcano' "), "The search," ("La ricerca"), "Strange type," ("Uno strano proto").

D45 *Caustico lunare.* [*Lunar Caustic.*] Translated by Vincenzo Mantovani. Milano: Arnoldo Mondadori, 1973. Issued in dust jacket.

D46 *Il traghetto per Gabriola.* [*October Ferry to Gabriola.*] Translated by Vincenzo Mantovani. Milano: Arnoldo Mondadori, 1974.

ANTHOLOGIES:

D47 *Carosello di narratori Inglese,* edited by Aldo Martello. Milan: Aldo Martello, 1954.
Contains Giorgio Monicelli's translation of "Strange Comfort Afforded by the Profession," ("I vanteggi del mestiere"), 273.

PERIODICALS:

D48 *Quaderni Milanesi,* Milan (Autumn 1960), 37.
Contains the short story "Elephant and Colosseum," ("Elefante e colosseo") translated by Giorgio Monicelli with an introduction by Emilio Tadini.

JAPANESE

BOOKS:

D49 *Kakkazan no shita.* [*Under the Volcano.*] Translated by Hideo Kano. Tokyo: Hakusuisha, 1966.

NORWEGIAN

BOOKS:

D50 *Under vulkanen.* [*Under the Volcano.*] Translated by Peter Magnus. Foreword by Sigurd Hoel. Oslo: Gyldendal Norsk Forlag, 1949. Issued in cloth with dust jacket and in paperback. Reissued in 1967. orange cloth backed orange boards,

POLISH

BOOKS:

D51 *Pod wulkanem.* [*Under the Volcano.*] Translated by Krystyna Tarnowska. Warsaw: Panstwowy Instytut Wydawniczy, 1963. Issued in dust jacket. Reissued in 1966 and 1976.

PERIODICALS:

D52 *Literatura na Swiecie,* Warsaw (no. 11, 1973), 56.
Contains *Lunar Caustic* translated by Jacek Laskowski.

PORTUGUESE

BOOKS:

D53 *Debaixo do vulcão.* [*Under the Volcano.*] Translated by Virginia Motta. Lisbon: Edicao Livros do Brasil, 1961.

D54 *Escuro como o túmulo onde jaz o meu amigo.* [*Dark as the Grave Wherein My Friend Is Laid.*] Translated by Carmen Gonzalez. Lisbon: Colecção Século XX, 1975.

D55 *Ouve-nos Senhor do Ceu que e a tua morada. Atraves do Canal do Panama.* [*Hear us O Lord in heaven thy dwelling place.*] Translated by Ana Hatherly. Lisbon: Iniciativas Editorials, 92, 1977.

RUSSIAN

BOOKS:

D56 *U podnoz'ja vulkana.* [*Under the Volcano.*] Translated by V. Hiñkis, I. Gurova & O. Soroka. Moscow: Progress, 1972.

ANTHOLOGIES:

D57 *Zateriannaia ulitsa: Sovremennaia kanadskaia novella* (*The Lost Street: The Contemporary Canadian Novella*) edited by N. Krolik. Moscow, Progress, 1971.
Contains "The Bravest Boat" ("Samaia khrabraia lodka"), 125, translated by the editor.

SERBO CROATIAN

BOOKS:

D58 *Ispod vulkana.* [*Under the Volcano.*] Translated by Branko Vućićević. Beograd: Nolit, 1966. Issued in unprinted acetate jacket. Reissued in 1975.

SLOVENIAN

BOOKS:

D59 *Pod ognjenikom.* [*Under the Volcano.*] Translated by Mira Mihelićeva. Ljubljana: Cankarjeva Založba, 1965. Issued in dust jacket.

SPANISH

BOOKS:

D60 *Bajo en volcán.* [*Under the Volcano.*] Translated by Raúl Ortiz y Ortiz. Mexico: Biblioteca Era, 1964. Reissued in 1970 and 1974. Also published by Editorial Galerna in Buenos Aires in 1967.

D61 *Ultramarina.* [*Ultramarine.*] Translated by Alfonso Llanos. Caracas: Monte Avila, 1969. Reissued 1970.

D62 *Oscuro como la tumba donde yace mi amigo.* [*Dark as the Grave Wherein My Friend Is Laid.*] Translated by Alicia Jurado. Caracas: Monte Avila, 1969.

D63 *Por el Canal de Panamá.* [*Through the Panama.*] Translated by Salvador Elizondo. Mexico: Ediciones Era, 1969.

D64 *Lunar Caustic.* Translated by R. E. Lorento. Prologo de Carlos Martinez Moreno. Montevideo: Editorial Alfa, 1970.

D65 *Escúchanos, oh Señor, desde el cielo, tu morada.* [*Hear us O Lord from heaven thy dwelling place*]. Translated by Eva Iribarne Dietrich. Caracas: Editorial Tiempo Nuevo, 1971.

D66 *El volcán, El mezcal, Los comisarios.* [*Selected Letters.*] Translated by Sergio Pitol. Barcelona: Tusquets, 1971.

PERIODICALS:

D67 *Revista de la Universidad de Mexico,* Mexico City, XVII, no. 2 (October 1962), 4–5.
Contains translations by Jaime Garcia Terrés of the poems "The volcano is dark," ("Esta negro el volcán"), "Delirium in Vera Cruz," ("Delirio en Veracruz") and "In the Oaxaca gaol," ("La cárcel de Oaxaca").

D68 *Mexico en la Cultura*, Mexico City (8 March 1964), 2
Contains Mario Beauregard's translation of "The Garden of Etla," ("El Jardin de Etla").

D69 *Revista de la Universidad de Mexico*, XIX, no. 3 (November 1964), 13–22.

Contains a translation of Lowry's letter of 15 June 1946 to his attorney A. Ronald Button concerning his imprisonment in Mexico. This issue also contains Bob Schaljkwijk's photographs of Quauhnáhuac (Cuernavaca) with quotations from Lowry as captions.

D70 *Revista Nacional de Cultura,* Mexico City, 186 (October/December 1968), 32–41.
Contains Alicia Jurado's translation of Douglas Day's preface to *Dark as the Grave Wherein My Friend Is Laid,* ("Malcolm Lowry: oscuro como la tumba donde mi amigo yace"). The preface contains quotations from the book as well as from several Lowry letters.

SWEDISH

BOOKS:

D71 *Under vulkanen.* [*Under the Volcano.*] Translated by Erik Sandin. Stockholm: Albert Bonniers Forlag, 1970.

PERIODICALS:

D72 *Bonniers Litterara Magasin,* Stockholm (no. 31, 1962), 285.
Contains a translation of "Through the Panama," ("Genom Panama"), by Sonja Bergvall.

TURKISH

BOOKS:

D73 *Yanardağ.* [*Under the Volcano.*] Translated by Aziz Üstel. Istanbul: Doyuran Matbaasi, 1974.

SECTION E
Radio, Television and Film

E. Radio, Television, and Film

E1 *Under the Volcano.* Radio adaptation, Columbia Broadcasting System, "Studio One," New York, 29 April 1947, 9:30–10:30 P.M. Writer/director: Fletcher Markle; producer: Robert J. Landry; script editor: Gerald Noxon; original music: Alexander Semmler. Consul: Everett Sloan; Yvonne: Anne Burr; Hugh: Hedley Rainnie; narrator: Joe de Santis. CBS does not have any tapes or scripts available from radio programs of the 1940s.

E2 *After the Volcano . . .* "CBC Wednesday Night." Canadian Broadcasting Corporation radio, 21 June 1961, 7:35–8:30 P.M. Produced by Jack Hutchinson; narration and script by Earle Birney. Combines readings from Lowry's published, and at that time unpublished, works by John Hardinge, with taped interviews with Margerie Lowry, Harvey Burt, Downie Kirk, and William McConnell. Lowry's song "On Such a May Morning" is sung by Dr. Jim Butler.

E3 *Remembrance of Lowry.* Two-part television program, Canadian Broadcasting Corporation, "Explorations," Vancouver, 22 and 29 November 1961, 10:30 P.M. Script by George Woodcock; produced by George Robertson. The first program, "To the Volcano," is an account of Lowry's life prior to his arrival in British Columbia; the second, "The Forest Path," tells of his productive period in Canada and his subsequent years in Europe shortly before his death in 1957. Interviews with many who knew Lowry and readings from his works by John Hardinge. Repeated 24 February and 2 March 1964.

E4 *Selected Poems of Malcolm Lowry* by John Peter. Radio program, Canadian Broadcasting Corporation, "Critics at Large," 11 September 1962. A review of *Selected Poems* (San Francisco: City Lights, 1962) quoting the poem "Hostage."

E5 *Rough Passage.* BBC-2 "New Release A magazine of the arts." British Broadcasting Corporation television, 2 February 1967, 10:20–10:49 P.M. Produced by Melvyn Bragg; introduced by Alex Glasgow. Interviews with Martin Case, Arthur Calder-Marshall, David Markson, Tom Maschler, Edwin Mason, Ronald Hill, John Moffatt, Charlotte Haldane, Philip Toynbee, Gerald Noxon, Harvey Breit, Earle Birney, Barbara Frum, Stuart Lowry, Conrad Aiken, John Davenport, and Sidney Belmont. Lowry's poems "Epitaph" and "Happiness" are read as well as excerpts from Charlotte Haldane's *I Bring Not Peace.* Repeated 8 June 1967, 10:26 P.M.

E6 *A Portrait of Malcolm Lowry* compiled by Arthur Calder-Marshall. Radio program, British Broadcasting Corporation, "Third Programme," 16 September 1967. Based on comments by various people who knew him (Conrad Aiken, Ian Parsons, James Stern, and others), the whole composed and narrated by Calder-Marshall. An edited version appears in *The Listener*, 12 October 1967.

E7 *Under the Volcano*. Film script by Melvyn Bragg based on the novel by Malcolm Lowry. 102 pages. The history of the film rights to Lowry's novel is complicated, but from papers in the collection of the bibliographer it appears that Margerie Lowry sold rights to "Volcano Productions Limited" in 1962. Some time later these rights were acquired by Harvey Breit and Ruth Ford Scott who in 1968 sold the rights to Robert and Raymond Hakim of "Paris Film Production." The Hakim brothers in 1972 were negotiating with Richard Burton to play the role of the consul in a film to be produced by Edward Dmytryck, and the script seems to have been written for this production. The film, however, was never produced. Copy of film script in collection of bibliographer.

E8 *The Bravest Boat.* Robert D. Graff wrote a film script of this short story in the early 1960s, but it was never produced. It was, however, quoted from in *Canadian Literature*, no. 44 (Spring 1970), 38–49 (*See* C218).

E9 "Day's Lowry." BBC Radio, 16 August 1974, 8:25 P.M. Arthur Calder-Marshall comments on Douglas Day's biography of Lowry in the light of his own meetings with Lowry in London and Mexico in the 1930s.

E10 "Books and Writers" (part of the program "Woman's Hour"), BBC Radio, 16 September 1974. Produced by Dorian Cooke and narrated by Chris Bickerton. Arthur Calder-Marshall disputes M. C. Bradbrook's version of Lowry's contact with Charlotte Haldane and doubts the "authenticity" of the later works.

Note: This information is taken from William H. New's *Malcolm Lowry A Reference Guide* (Boston: G. K. Hall & Co., 1978). The BBC, although most helpful, has not been able to supply any information on this program.

E11 *Volcano: An Inquiry into the Life of Malcolm Lowry.* A documentary film written by Donald Brittain with John Kramer. Produced by Donald Brittain and R. A. Duncan for the National Film Board of Canada. Narrated by Donald Brittain, with words of Malcolm Lowry spoken by Richard Burton. Director of photography, Douglas Kiefer; edited by John Kramer; music by Alain Clavier. First broadcast on the Canadian Broadcasting Corporation television network on 7 April 1976. Made on location in Canada, England, and Mexico, the film interviews 44 people about Lowry and quotes extensively from *Under the Volcano.* Nominated for an Academy Award in 1977 in the feature documentary category. Entered also in the 19th American Film Festival (New York, 1977), it won first prize in the feature length arts category. 100 minutes. Copy of script in collection of the bibliographer.

E12 *Under the Volcano.* Radio adaptation, British Broadcasting Corporation, "Hi-Fi Theatre," London, 9 March 1979, 3:05–5:00 P.M. Repeated 12 and 15 March 1979. Adapted for radio by Eric Ewens; music by Graham Collier; directed by John Tydeman. Lowry (as narrator): Paul Scofield; Dr. Arturo Vigil: William Fox; Jacques Laruelle: David March; Emperor Maximilian: Philip Voss; Empress Carlotta: Eva Stuart; Signor Bustamente: Trader Faulkner; Geoffrey Firmin: Norman Rodway; Yvonne: June Tobin; Hugh: Denys Hawthorne; Familiar 1: Leonard Fenton; Familiar 2: John Bull; Everard: Gordon Dulieu; Cervantes: Gregory de Polnay; Dios: Andrew Branch; Maria: Eva Stuart; Policeman: John Bull. Copy of script in collection of bibliographer.

SECTION F
Song Lyrics

F. Song Lyrics

F1 *Three Little Dog-Gone Mice Just the Latest Charleston Fox-Trot Ever.* Lyrics by Malcolm Lowry; music by Ronald Hill. London, Worton David Ltd. Published 1927 at 6*d*. Publisher's records not available. See illustration.

F2 *I've Said Good-Bye to Shanghai.* Vocal Fox-Trot (with ukulele accompt.). Lyrics by Malcolm Lowry; music by Ronald Hill. London, B. Feldman & Co. Published 1927 at 6*d* Publisher's records not available. See illustration.

Note: The following song lyrics, "And when I die it'll be just the same," "Give me the money," "Here is all the music that's within my soul," and "Rich man, poor man, beggarman, thief," are quoted in Charlotte Haldane's *I Bring Not Peace*, London, Chatto & Windus, 1932 (B3). For Lowry's song "On Such a May Morning," see E2.

SECTION G
Recordings

G. Recordings

G1 *Symphony of Scorpions/Forest Path to the Spring* (instrumental only). Composed by Graham Collier. Mosaic Records GCM 773. 1 33⅓ rpm 12-inch stereo recording.

Symphony of Scorpions features Art Themen (soprano and tenor saxophones), Harry Beckett, Henry Lowther, and Peter Duncan (trumpets), Malcolm Griffiths (trombone), Tony Roberts and Mike Page (saxophones), Ed Speight (guitar), Roger Dean (piano), John Webb (drums), John Mitchell (percussion), and Graham Collier (bass and leader). Recorded at Ronnie Scott's Club, London, 7 November 1976.

Forest Path to the Spring features Art Themen (soprano and tenor saxophones), and Ed Speight (acoustic guitar). Recorded 10 March 1977.

Note: Study scores were available for this and the following recordings but these are at present out of print and have not been seen by the bibliographer.

G2 *The Day of the Dead/October Ferry.* Based on the words of Malcolm Lowry with music by Graham Collier. Mosaic Records GCMD 783/4. 2 33⅓ rpm 12-inch recordings. Recorded March/April 1978 in Nettlebed, Oxfordshire.

The Day of the Dead: Words from *Under the Volcano, Dark as the Grave Wherein My Friend Is Laid, Forest Path to the Spring*, and *Selected Letters.* Narrated by John Carbery and performed by Alan Wakeman (tenor and soprano saxophones and bass clarinet), Art Themen (tenor and soprano saxophones), Roger Dean (acoustic and electric piano), Ed Speight (acoustic and electric guitar), Roy Babbington (acoustic and electric bass), Ashley Brown (drums and percussion), Alan Jackson (drums), Malcolm Griffiths (trombone), Mike Page (alto and soprano saxophones), Henry Lowther, Harry Beckett, and Peter Duncan (trumpet & flugel), and Graham Collier (direction and additional keyboards). First performed in Ilkley King's Hall, 9 June 1977.

Note: Part VII was originally recorded without narration as *Forest Path to the Spring* on *Symphony of Scorpions* (G1).

October Ferry (instrumental only) featuring the same musicians as *The Day of the Dead* but without Ashley Brown and Alan Jackson. First performed Budapest, Hungary, 9 September 1977.

INDEX

References are to item numbers. Poems are in quotations with only the first letter of the first word capitalized. Short stories and articles are in quotations with the first letter of each word capitalized. Titles of books, by Lowry or by others, are in small caps, as are the titles of radio and television programs and recordings. Published letters from Lowry, with the exception of those in *Selected Letters*, are indexed under "Letters to" followed by the names of the recipients in alphabetical order.